"This is a good book. It encourages our souls to know that those greatly used by God often experience seasons of depression, persecution, sorrow, and suffering. It reminds us that God draws near most often when we are down and hurting, not when we are up and prospering. Many will be blessed by these portraits. I know I was."

Daniel L. Akin

"Collin Hansen and Jeff Robinson have presented to us more than the usual suspects of pastoral ministry in the history of the church. Several of the individuals included in this volume were unknown to me before reading the book. But each of them, in his own way, is a Christ-exalting portrait of both the suffering and the joy that God has called us to embrace as pastors. I highly recommend it!"

Sam Storms, Bridgeway Church, Oklahoma City, OK

"This remarkable book goes ahead in time to gather foretastes of heavenly joy and pours them out in chapter after chapter of clear, compelling testimony. Everyone who reads *12 Faithful Men* will be strengthened, convicted, and instructed by these skillfully crafted chapters. This book made me long for our heavenly future and yearn for earthly faithfulness."

Andrew M. Davis, senior pastor, First Baptist Church, Durham, NC

"Suffering in the ministry is a distinguishing mark of a true servant of God. Yet we are often surprised and disillusioned when it comes upon us. *12 Faithful Men* provides help in this regard as it surveys some of the greatest men in church history and the afflictions they suffered in their personal ministries. We are familiar with their successes, but what do we know about their afflictions? Here is much-needed encouragement for all who serve God and are sailing the turbulent waters of gospel ministry."

Steven J. Lawson, president of OnePassion Ministries, Dallas, TX

"Historically rooted, biblically sound, and biographically diverse, this book shows that the road of biblical faithfulness is one marked by pain and suffering. Whether we are new to the pastorate or veteran shepherds, this work—which elucidates the stories of suffering and the faithfulness of the saints that have gone before us—reminds us that we are not anomalies but that every man of God will be tested often. I'm thankful for this breath of fresh air."

Jamaal Williams, lead pastor, Sojourn
Community Church—Midtown

"The pathway to the beatific vision often entails suffering and heartache. And this is especially true of the pilgrimages of those called to vocational ministry. This volume, which recounts the lives of twelve such ministers of the gospel from all over the globe and throughout the history of the church, is a terrific reminder of the cost of faithfulness in the service of the Lord of glory. An excellent resource."

Michael A. G. Haykin, professor of church history and biblical
spirituality, Southern Baptist Theological Seminary

"*12 Faithful Men* was conceived in the throes of deep spiritual testing. The editors and each of the contributors have experienced the sanctifying fires of God's providence about which they write. The subjects chosen for discussion come from a variety of denominations, ethnicities, nationalities, and circumstances. Their particular contexts of tribulation cover a great diversity of ways in which God allows his servants to be assaulted. Under the power of this diversity, the united experience is one of divine faithfulness. This book demonstrates that Christian ministry and Christian life consist in suffering. Suffering is not an appendage simply to be endured or overcome but is the essence of knowing Christ and communicating the life of Christ in this world."

Tom J. Nettles, senior professor, Southern Baptist
Theological Seminary

"Church leadership comes with a cross and invites all pastors to be impaled upon it. But you now hold a healing balm for when the hammer strikes. Through extraordinary stories of ministerial affliction, *12 Faithful Men* prepares leaders for suffering and encourages leaders in suffering!"

Dave Harvey, president of Sojourn Network; teaching pastor, Summit Church; founder of Amicalled.com; and author

"Faithful pastoral ministry will inevitably include hardship and temptations to discouragement. None of us is exempt. So who of us does not stand in need of the regular encouragement of seeing others live out their pastoral ministries with persevering faithfulness? I experienced that encouragement many times as I read the chapters of this book. Let this book provide that encouragement for you."

Mike Bullmore, senior pastor, CrossWay Community Church, Bristol, WI

"Aside from God's Word and prayer, reading biographies has been the most useful goad and guide to endurance when trials dog my steps. In the most difficult times, the story of a brother faithfully enduring gave me courage to continue on. By putting twelve of these stories together, Collin Hansen and Jeff Robinson have done an enormous favor to those engaged in ministry. Some familiar and others less so, these biographical sketches prove to be just the balm to salve wounds and energize the spirit to press on in faithfulness. This book is a *go to* for encouragement to endure."

Phil A. Newton, senior pastor, South Woods Baptist Church, Memphis, TN; author of *The Mentoring Church: How Pastors and Congregations Cultivate Leaders*

"The apostle Paul called Timothy, his 'son,' to 'imitate me as I imitate Christ.' One of the great blessings of God's providence is the record of godly men who with their lives point us to Christ and give us insights on how we can effectively lead others to Christ. In this volume, Collin and Jeff have given us a treasury to draw from that contains inspiration, instruction, and Christ-honoring motivation. Enjoy it and share it."

Harry L. Reeder III, pastor teacher, Briarwood Presbyterian Church, Birmingham, AL

"In *12 Faithful Men*, Collin Hansen and Jeff Robinson have written a deeply challenging and profoundly encouraging account of pastors who learned that the pastoral life is the Christoform life, one marked by suffering as well as glory. Their book tells the story of widely varied men, all profoundly wounded, faithful, and fruitful in the Lord's work."

Dan Doriani, vice president of strategic academic projects and professor of theology and ethics at Covenant Theological Seminary, St. Louis, MO

12 FAITHFUL MEN

12 FAITHFUL MEN

*Portraits of Courageous Endurance
in Pastoral Ministry*

COLLIN HANSEN and JEFF ROBINSON, EDS.

BakerBooks

a division of Baker Publishing Group
Grand Rapids, Michigan

Published by Baker Books
a division of Baker Publishing Group
PO Box 6287, Grand Rapids, MI 49516-6287
www.bakerbooks.com

Printed in the United States of America

Library of Congress Cataloging-in-Publication Data
Names: Hansen, Collin, 1981– editor.
Title: 12 faithful men : portraits of courageous endurance in pastoral ministry /
    Collin Hansen and Jeff Robinson, editors.
Other titles: Twelve faithful men
Description: Grand Rapids : Baker Publishing Group, 2018.
Identifiers: LCCN 2017059998 | ISBN 9780801077760 (pbk.)
Subjects: LCSH: Suffering—Religious aspects—Christianity. | Christian biography.
Classification: LCC BV4909 .A14 2018 | DDC 270.092/2 [B] —dc23
LC record available at https://lccn.loc.gov/2017059998

In keeping with biblical principles of creation stewardship, Baker Publishing Group advocates the responsible use of our natural resources. As a member of the Green Press Initiative, our company uses recycled paper when possible. The text paper of this book is composed in part of post-consumer waste.

18   19   20   21   22   23   24   7   6   5   4   3   2   1

CONTENTS

Contents

FOREWORD

Young pastors today are often cool, impressive, and popular. But the pastoral ministry that has borne eternal fruit down through the centuries has been something deeper, grander, and more resilient. The apostle Paul expresses it when he writes, "I rejoice in my sufferings for your sake" (Col. 1:24). Paul was not cool. He had something better. Into his pastoral ministry flowed two divine powers: suffering and rejoicing.

It is not enough that we pastors today suffer as Paul did. We must suffer without self-pity, resentment, or murmuring but with rejoicing. Then we advance the gospel. How could it be otherwise? We represent the One "who for the joy that was set before him endured the cross" (Heb. 12:2).

As a young pastor, I entered the ministry prepared for the rejoicing but not for the suffering. When the inevitable buffetings and sorrows came, especially in the form of rejection, I thought, *I don't deserve this.* Maybe you've thought that too. And while it is a valid thought, it is not profound.

11

As the Lord led me further along, the following verses, like so many throughout Scripture, became more meaningful to me:

I am sending you out as lambs in the midst of wolves. (Luke 10:3)

Whoever kills you will think he is offering service to God. (John 16:2)

I have been crucified with Christ. (Gal. 2:20)

Do not be surprised at the fiery trial. (1 Pet. 4:12)

I am filling up what is lacking in Christ's afflictions for the sake of his body, that is, the church. (Col. 1:24)

The Lord did not recruit pastors on false pretenses. He told us what to expect. We will suffer, for his sake. But for that very reason, because it is for him, our sufferings are a grace, a privilege, an honor he is giving us. We are following him down a path already stained with his priceless blood. When we realize this, a second thought breaks upon us: *I really don't deserve this.* And that is profound, and it leads to profound rejoicing.

The privilege of pastoral ministry is *Jesus*—serving Jesus, standing for Jesus, representing Jesus, laying down our lives for Jesus, and through it all knowing Jesus more deeply. As my dad, the best pastor I've ever known, told me on his dying day: "Ministry isn't everything. Jesus is."

Collin Hansen and Jeff Robinson have gathered together godly pastors to tell us stories, true stories, of pastoral suffering with rejoicing that bears fruit to last forever. We pastors of today can never say the Lord is asking too much of us. The pastors we read of here proved that Jesus is worth it all, even to our hearts' full rejoicing forever.

Ray Ortlund
Immanuel Church
Nashville, Tennessee
August 28, 2017

ONE

PAUL: Apostle of Pastoral Affliction

JEFF ROBINSON

I f you sent a résumé to a search committee to be considered for a pastoral opening, what types of information would it contain? No doubt it would detail all the positive ministry experience you have logged. If you had served as a pastor in one place for a few years, you'd put that first, particularly if things went fairly well. If you worked as a youth minister while in college, you'd put that down. If you taught a Bible class or served a short-term mission stint overseas, that would certainly make the list. You would include the names and contact information for several people likely to give a friendly assessment of your qualifications, character, and background.

Your aim would be to make certain your strengths stand out in bold relief so you would appear—on paper at least—better qualified than the other candidates.

A band of "super-apostles" forced the apostle Paul to brandish his ministry credentials late in his second letter to the church at Corinth. Thus, in 2 Corinthians 11, Paul provided his pastoral résumé, boasting in a rather lengthy set of qualifications that authenticated him as an apostle called and inspired by God. What made Paul's ministry vitae?

> Are they servants of Christ? I am a better one—I am talking like a madman—with far greater labors, far more imprisonments, with countless beatings, and often near death. Five times I received at the hands of the Jews the forty lashes less one. Three times I was beaten with rods. Once I was stoned. Three times I was shipwrecked; a night and a day I was adrift at sea; on frequent journeys, in danger from rivers, danger from robbers, danger from my own people, danger from Gentiles, danger in the city, danger in the wilderness, danger at sea, danger from false brothers; in toil and hardship, through many a sleepless night, in hunger and thirst, often without food, in cold and exposure. And, apart from other things, there is the daily pressure on me of my anxiety for all the churches. Who is weak, and I am not weak? Who is made to fall, and I am not indignant? If I must boast, I will boast of the things that show my weakness. (vv. 23–30)

Paul's ministry qualifications read like the diary of an Auschwitz survivor: imprisonment on false charges, flogging, starvation, shipwrecked, hard labor, robbed, sleepless nights—all things that portray him as a weak man. Why? Because, as Paul goes on to tell the Corinthians in chapter 12, he was called to suffer. The gospel's work moves forward and the church gets built on the tracks of suffering, which demonstrate God's power working through the conduit of human frailty. When I am tempted to throw a pity party over some trifling anguish I'm facing in ministry, I go to Paul's account here to put it in perspective. I will never suffer this way for Christ. Compared to this, all is well.

It is clear from Paul's writing in 2 Corinthians and in other epistles that he expected all faithful ministers to experience some level of affliction. In 2 Timothy 2:3, Paul commanded that Timothy, his son in the faith, "share in suffering as a good soldier of Christ Jesus."

As a herald of the gospel of Jesus Christ, I am called to suffer.

Suffering: Normative for Pastors

Throughout the history of the church of Jesus Christ, a pattern has emerged. Those whom God has used profoundly to build his church suffered grinding affliction along the way. The church father Athanasius (AD 296–373) was exiled five times on accusations of heresy. Dozens of early believers were burned at the stake or fed to lions. John Calvin (1509–64) lived much of his life under a threat of death from the Roman Catholic Church. Puritan pastor John Bunyan (1628–88) wrote *Pilgrim's Progress* during a twelve-year imprisonment for preaching the gospel. Charles Spurgeon (1834–92) lived in constant physical pain and suffered profound anxiety for boldly upholding God's Word in the face of rising liberalism in the nineteenth century.

Scores of others, including those whose stories compose the remaining chapters of this book, lived out the famous dictum of A. W. Tozer (1897–1963): "It is doubtful whether God can bless a man greatly until he has hurt him deeply."[1]

That is essentially the thesis of this book—before (or often while) God uses his ministers, he first fits them for gospel work with a harrowing walk along the Calvary Road of suffering. The apostle Paul is something of a biblical paradigm of the suffering pastor. He detailed affliction in many of his letters, but teased it out in the greatest depth in 2 Corinthians. This chapter will make six arguments, mostly from Paul's witness in 2 Corinthians, to show how God employs suffering not only to fit his ministers for gospel ministry but also to proclaim that same gospel of grace to a lost and dying world.

Tom Schreiner crystalizes Paul's self-understanding well:

> We should not conceive of Paul as engaging in mission and experiencing the unfortunate consequence of suffering in the process, as if his difficulties were unrelated to his mission. On the contrary, the pain Paul endured was the means by which the message of the gospel was extended to the nations. Suffering was not a side effect of the Pauline mission; rather it was at the very center of his apostolic evangelism. His distress validated and legitimated his message, demonstrating the truth of the gospel.[2]

God promised Paul suffering in Acts 9:15–16, "But the Lord said to [Ananias], 'Go, for he is a chosen instrument of mine to carry my name before the Gentiles and kings and the children of Israel. For I will show him how much he must suffer for the sake of my name.'"

It is vital that ministers recognize this promise early in their ministries, else they may be tempted to quit when things don't go as planned. Suffering will either confirm their calling or drive them from ministry.

Pastors in the Hands of an Angry God?

When a season of suffering sets in, pastors tend to wonder if something in the cosmos is out of kilter. Perhaps God is angry with me. Maybe his hand is not on my ministry. Maybe I need to microexamine myself as a young Martin Luther did to see if undetected sin has caused God to write "Ichabod" over the door of my life and ministry.

The super-apostles seemed to believe Paul's troubles were ironclad evidence of God's displeasure with him; surely one who boasts in such things as floggings and hunger has lost his mind and has, in fact, been abandoned by God. But Paul argued nothing could be further from the truth. Instead, affliction might provide key evidence that God is, in fact, with his ministers. Through suffering, Paul learned six key lessons about faithfulness every pastor ought to take to heart early in their ministry.

Paul's Suffering Taught Him How to Minister Gospel Compassion to Others

Blessed be the God and Father of our Lord Jesus Christ, the Father of mercies and God of all comfort, who comforts us in all our affliction, so that we may be able to comfort those who are in any affliction, with the comfort with which we ourselves are comforted by God. For as we share abundantly in Christ's sufferings, so through Christ we share abundantly in comfort too. If we are afflicted, it is for your comfort and salvation; and if we are comforted, it is for your comfort, which you experience when you patiently endure the same sufferings that we suffer. Our hope for you is unshaken, for we know that as you share in our sufferings, you will also share in our comfort. (2 Cor. 1:3–7)

My wife and I had never been able to relate to the many families around us who suffered through failed pregnancies until our first son died in Lisa's womb in the fall of 1999 after five months. We were planning on naming him after my distant cousin, baseball great Brooks Robinson, in hopes God would give him that same baseball gene. In the years that followed, we were amazed at how many friends came to us for counsel and encouragement after losing a child in utero.

I had never really been able to relate to fellow pastors whose ministries exploded like Mount Vesuvius until mine did two years into my first pastorate. Previously, the best I could do was offer some Reformed-sounding platitudes featuring the Puritans, Spurgeon, and maybe Corrie ten Boom, assuring them that these saints suffered and we must too. But my words fell with a thud; I knew not of what I spoke.

We don't fully understand affliction and God's unbending faithfulness in the cauldron until we've spent time boiling in it. God remedies this lack in his servants as the apostle learned ad nauseam. Paul and Barnabas strengthened the churches at Derbe, Lystra, Iconium, and Pisidian Antioch and instructed Christians to remain true to Christ, assuring them "that through many tribulations we must enter the kingdom of God" (Acts 14:22). How were they to become kingdom citizens? Surely through Christ alone but also through trials. But Paul assured his readers that God would be with them in the furnace—as he had the Hebrew boys in Daniel 3. In turn, they would then be able to assure anxious believers of the faithfulness, love, and mercy of God who promised never to leave nor forsake his people (Heb. 13:5).

Pastoral ministry is not a shelter from the storm of this fallen world. Rather, it is a call to plunge headlong into it.

God calls his servants to run to the battle, not away from it. And God sees us through difficult times so we can provide the sheep with the comfort that comes from trusting fully in the kind purposes of the good shepherd. Calvin rightly refers to this as "the fellowship of suffering."[3]

Just as the disciples picked up twelve baskets full of leftovers at the feeding of the five thousand, Jesus will not waste your suffering. He will use it to make you a compassionate shepherd in the local church for his glory as you experience the same aspects of the fallen world as do members of your congregation.

God's fashioning of his leaders through affliction is the gospel-centered path to maturity. Don Carson asserts: "The most mature Christian leaders want to absorb an additional share of sufferings so that their flocks may correspondingly be spared some suffering. In this, they imitate Christ."[4]

Paul's Suffering Demonstrated Human Weakness and the Power of God

But we have this treasure in jars of clay, to show that the surpassing power belongs to God and not to us. We are afflicted in every way, but not crushed; perplexed, but not driven to despair; persecuted, but not forsaken; struck down, but not destroyed. (2 Cor. 4:7–9)

There is nothing fetching about paper plates—even those with "heavy duty" stamped on the package. They are utilitarian, designed for a single purpose—to hold food and allow the user to successfully consume the food. Then they are thrown in the garbage.

In 2 Corinthians 4:7, Paul says pastors are kind of like cheap crockery—mere clay pots. God uses them to display and deploy a precious and powerful message—the gospel. Through this ordinary means, God proclaims his extraordinary gospel to show that the meal, and not the plate, ultimately nourishes believers.

And the clay pots are vessels God subjects to suffering. But he brings them through it unspoiled and intact to demonstrate that the power to save sinners and preserve pastors belongs entirely to him.

Paul endured all manner of physical affliction, which he cataloged in verses 8–9, adding that because of God's grace, none of them destroyed him: "Afflicted in every way, but not crushed; perplexed, but not driven to despair; persecuted, but not forsaken; struck down, but not destroyed." Like Paul, all human heralds are weak, but God's power is not short-circuited by their weakness.

Why did God strike Paul with such angry waves? "To show that the surpassing power belongs to God and not to us." By suffering on behalf of his Lord, Paul carries in his body the dying of Jesus. In Galatians 6:17, Paul makes clear that he bears in his body "the marks of Jesus." Schreiner comments on this passage: "Paul's commitment to suffer and die for Christ is the means by which the strength of Jesus and his life are revealed through Paul."[5]

John Bunyan, whom you will encounter in a later chapter, illustrates this point particularly well. The Puritan preacher was arrested in 1661 for preaching in a service outside the officially sanctioned state church. He spent twelve years in a squalid Bedford jail and wrote many great works, including *Pilgrim's Progress*, the second bestselling book of all time after the Bible. Bunyan was not an educated man. He never spent a single day in seminary. He was a tinker—a repairer of pots and pans—who ministered in the rural town of Bedford, England. Yet God continues to speak to millions today through his printed works. A powerful man? No. A clay pot? Yes. When told he could go home if he promised to stop preaching Christ as a separatist minister, Bunyan reportedly responded, "If I were out of prison today, I would preach the gospel again tomorrow by the help of God."[6]

By human reckoning, God's entire project of redemption appears weak. Jesus was born in a lowly stable to unremarkable parents and lived an obscure life. He was eventually nailed to a cross between two thieves and buried in a borrowed tomb. Many throughout history have dismissed Christianity and its crucified Christ as a weak religion for weak people.

Indeed, in one important sense, these critics are correct. Like Paul, like the tinker of Bedford, all of us are clay pots, weak people. If sinners will be transformed, God must do it. And he will strike the clay pot along the way to prepare it for difficult work.

God saved sinners through the affliction of his apostle. But he also made Paul's feet stand firm in the midst of it all. Paul expresses this dynamic in a series of contrasting couplets: he was afflicted in every way, but not crushed; perplexed, but not driven to despair; persecuted, but not forsaken; struck down, but not destroyed. My favorite is the second one: "perplexed, but not driven to despair." I have often been perplexed in the ministry. What is God doing? Why is he doing it this way? More times than not, I've been mystified at God's ways. But each time I have come to Paul's words here. Like drinking water from an oasis in a desert, I drew fresh stores of grace from "but not driven to despair" and was refreshed to persevere.

God's servants will suffer, but he will not let them go. He is demonstrating his awesome power through their astonishing powerlessness.

Paul's Suffering Illustrated the Gospel He Was Called to Proclaim

[We are] always carrying in the body the death of Jesus, so that the life of Jesus may also be manifested in our bodies. For we who live are always being given over to death for Jesus' sake, so that the life of Jesus also may be manifested in our mortal flesh. So death is at work in us, but life in you. (2 Cor. 4:10–12)

I'm not a big fan of the aphorism often (and erroneously) attributed to St. Francis of Assisi: "Preach the gospel at all times, use words if necessary." It's a well-intended cliché, but God has commanded gospel heralds to use words. He has invested his Word with transforming power. Paul's call to proclaim Christ certainly required words, but to his mind it also entailed something else: a willingness to die for Christ. For Paul, gospel proclamation was a call to both preach and die because the words were illustrated by (and explained) the actions.

Paul was committed to suffer and die for the cause of Christ, and such a willingness turned out to be the means by which the death of Jesus was revealed through Paul. The super-apostles argued that signs and wonders were certain proof that the Spirit of God was at work. But Paul maintained that one must suffer for the life and death of Jesus to be illustrated. God was using Paul's suffering as an agent of life in the Corinthians. Schreiner writes, "Paul is again, therefore, the corollary of Jesus, for just as Jesus died to convey life to his people, so too Paul must suffer for the life of God to be communicated to others."[7]

The apostle was willing to sacrifice his own life to see the Corinthians converted, thereby providing a living parable of the very good news he preached. Death was coming to Paul's body, but life was coming to the Corinthians through Christ. Contrary to the teaching of the super-apostles and their modern-day successors in the prosperity movement, every faithful gospel minister must be willing to sacrifice their life for the sake of the call to preach Christ. Acts 20:24 is something of a ministry manifesto for Paul: "I do not count my life of any value nor as precious to myself, if only I may finish my course and the ministry that I received from the Lord Jesus, to testify to the gospel of the grace of God." We see this lived out in 2 Corinthians.

Paul's doctrine here came home to me during the final weeks of my first pastorate. My church faced a terrible financial crisis. It could no longer afford my salary. I could find neither supplementary work nor full-time employment. After many weeks of prayer and counsel from other godly, wise men, I realized my only option was to resign. This text suddenly loomed large on the landscape of my life—was I willing to lay down even the ministry? In my farewell sermon, I preached John 12:24: "Unless a grain of wheat falls into the earth and dies, it remains alone; but if it dies, it bears much fruit." I prayed the congregation would see my point—I was seeking to live out Paul's words in 2 Corinthians 4:10–12. It was painful, and in many ways it left me perplexed, but it wound up allowing the church to continue to exist.

As Paul's ministry proved, and as I pray my actions in some small way affirmed, suffering does not deny the gospel but confirms its truthfulness.

Paul's Suffering Was a Means of Reorienting His Gaze to Eternal Things

So we do not lose heart. Though our outer self is wasting away, our inner self is being renewed day by day. For this light momentary affliction is preparing for us an eternal weight of glory beyond all comparison, as we look not to the things that are seen but to the things that are unseen. For the things that are seen are transient, but the things that are unseen are eternal. (2 Cor. 4:16–18)

As fallen humans, we tend to live for the moment. Our lives shrink down to the spontaneous thoughts, emotions, or needs that dominate our lives at a given place and time. Every crisis, no matter how small, can take on weight that far outstrips its true significance. As Paul David Tripp puts it:

In a moment, your thoughts can seem more important than they actually are. In a moment, your emotions can seem more reliable than they really are. In a moment, your needs can seem more essential than they truly are. . . . It's hard to live with eternity in view. Life does shrink to the moment again and again.[8]

This type of thinking often leads a pastor down the dark road of discouragement and through the doors of the dungeon of discontentment. A single email, text message, or phone call from a church member or deacon can push him into a mental spiral that leads to ten thousand speculative disasters. Or an offhand comment from an elder about his preaching can cause the man to question his call to ministry.

Pastors are an insecure lot. Like all sons of Adam, they easily succumb to the world's pressure to succeed. Faithfulness is the biblical barometer of success in ministry, but the siren song of the world with its chorus of "more, faster, bigger, shinier" often clouds the mind of God's man.

In his mercy, God rescues his undershepherds from these dangerous roads by reorienting their gaze from temporal things to heavenly things. In Paul's ministry, affliction was the instrument God employed to redirect the apostle's focus. Though he suffered grievously, as the laundry list of trials in 2 Corinthians 11 shows, Paul dismissed his terrible circumstances as "light momentary affliction."

Multiple imprisonments for the cause of Christ? Light momentary affliction.

Countless beatings? Light momentary affliction.

Often near death in service of the gospel? Light momentary affliction.

Shipwrecked three times? Light momentary affliction.

Adrift at sea a day and a night? Light momentary affliction.

Often without food and water in cold and exposure? Light momentary affliction.

Under a threat of death from Jews and Gentiles alike? Light momentary affliction.

God did not waste Paul's affliction; it was the catalyst that took his eyes off this world and fixed them on another. Suffering stamped eternity on Paul's eyeballs and enabled him to see that this world is a dress rehearsal for another.

Paraphrasing Charles Spurgeon, the Lord's mercy often rides to the door of our hearts on the black stallion of affliction. Through suffering, God gave Paul eyes to see the dangerous, uncertain, transitory nature of the kingdom of humankind over against the glorious, certain, eternal nature of the kingdom of God. Compared to the glories of another realm, the personal disasters of this one are nothing.

Paul's Suffering Proved the Integrity of His Ministry

But as servants of God we commend ourselves in every way: by great endurance, in afflictions, hardships, calamities, beatings, imprisonments, riots, labors, sleepless nights, hunger; by purity, knowledge, patience, kindness, the Holy Spirit, genuine love; by truthful speech, and the power of God; with the weapons of righteousness for the right hand and for the left; through honor and dishonor, through slander and praise. We are treated as impostors, and yet are true; as unknown, and yet well known; as dying, and behold, we live; as punished, and yet not killed; as sorrowful, yet always rejoicing; as poor, yet making many rich; as having nothing, yet possessing everything. (2 Cor. 6:4–10)

My dear friend and ministry hero Harry Reeder often says, "Circumstances do not shape character; they reveal it." In 1 Thessalonians 1:5, Paul says his response to suffering showed the kind of man he was because only a Spirit-empowered person could suffer with joy, trusting that God had ordained his circumstances for good. Such joy could only be produced by the Spirit of God (v. 6). Paul was an authentic, Spirit-filled, divinely called herald of God.

Schreiner rightly argues that the effectiveness of the message relies heavily upon the integrity of the messenger: "The effectiveness of the message of the cross is evacuated if the messengers are hucksters. On the other hand, proclaiming the gospel with integrity in the midst of suffering commends the gospel to the hearers."[9]

Indeed.

Second Corinthians 6 is another curriculum vitae setting forth Paul's ministerial qualifications. There, he lists ten elements of suffering in verses 4–5, then follows in verses 6–7 with nine elements of holiness.[10] In verses 8–10, he toggles back to nine additional types of suffering he's experienced. Paul's ministry is not so much validated by affliction as by the holiness it produces.

Just as the presence of semitrucks and other heavy vehicles will eventually reveal the cracks in the bulwark of a rusting, decaying bridge, so will extended bouts of affliction unmask a fake Christian or a false teacher. Paul had been broken, bruised, and battered. God's grace caused him to stand anyway, thus proving his calling as a genuine apostle of God.

Seminary students and pastoral interns often ask me to help authenticate and discern their calling. Certainly we consult the qualifications of elders in 1 Timothy 3 and Titus 1. But one certain indicator that God has called a man is that he stands firm and perseveres in ministry after he has been thoroughly buffeted by a hurricane of affliction. Paul suffered profoundly but pressed on in planting churches and proclaiming the gospel. This, he told the church at Corinth, separated him from the super-apostles. It proved the integrity and authenticity of his ministry.

The men profiled in subsequent chapters of this volume give further credence to Spurgeon's notion. Calvin was run out of Geneva but continued in the ministry until his death. Like Paul, Bunyan was jailed but wrote the second-most-famous Christian book in history from behind bars and later returned to shepherd his flock. Charles Simeon persevered in the face of a congregation that despised him.

Paul's Suffering Served as Dynamite That Destroyed Self-Glory

So to keep me from becoming conceited because of the surpassing greatness of the revelations, a thorn was given me in the flesh, a messenger of Satan to harass me, to keep me from becoming conceited. Three times I pleaded with the Lord about this, that it should leave me. But he said to me, "My grace is sufficient for you, for my power is made perfect in weakness." Therefore I will boast all the more gladly of my weaknesses, so that the power of Christ may rest upon me. For the sake of Christ, then, I am content with weaknesses, insults, hardships, persecutions, and calamities. For when I am weak, then I am strong. (2 Cor. 12:7–10)

Few Christians in the history of the church have experienced an encounter with God on a par with what Paul discusses in 2 Corinthians 12. Yet such an ecstatic vision of another world did not bolster Paul's pride—the vision slayed it. How? After God gave Paul a preview of heaven, he afflicted the apostle with what Paul called a "thorn in my flesh." Scripture is not clear as to the thorn's identity, but it was given for Paul's humility, to remind him that all his strength comes from the grace of God and not from himself. The thorn was God's loving dynamite that destroyed Paul's will to self-glory.[11]

Such a vision would certainly tempt even the most mature man of God toward seeking his own glory. Tweet it out, Facebook it, offer it as a "praise report" at church, shout it from the rooftops. But the parasite of self-glory—so endemic to fallen human beings—drains the lifeblood and ultimately buries authentic gospel ministry. Self-glory builds self-kingdoms, but it also brings opposition from God: "God opposes the proud but gives grace to the humble" (1 Pet. 5:5).

Paul realized that one of the most important weapons a pastor must possess in ministry is humility. The problem is none of us is naturally humble. Thus, God in his grace gives us thorns to wage war on self-glory and promote humility.

It may be an irascible deacon board, a physical malady (many think that was Paul's issue), a prodigal son, slim financial resources, depression and anxiety, cancer, the tragic death of your spouse or child, or any of a thousand other devastating realities. While our thorns may vary, God's intent is the same—to humble us and to remind us of our utter dependence on him.

And like Paul, you may fervently and repeatedly pray for removal from your circumstances, but God will not change them due to a larger and infinitely more glorious plan that you do not see—namely, your decreasing and his increasing. And God will give you something even greater than removal of the thorn: his strength that shines through your weakness.

God exposed my weakness and exploded my self-glory early in the ministry. My first pastorate lasted barely three years. At times, it was a nightmare. One of my elders falsely accused me of wrongdoing. A woman in the church plotted to plant pornography in my vehicle (overheard and confronted by another member, thankfully). Seven families conspired to have me removed and replaced with a more "reformed" man. Two weeks before I resigned, another elder called for a vote of confidence before the entire congregation (mercifully, they rejected his attempt) as my wife and children watched from the second row. There were thorns galore. But from the vantage point of a few years, I see how God used all of them to show me his power and my weakness. In ministry as in all things, all glory belongs to him alone.

Grueling, Glorious Calling

Sarah Eekhoff Zylstra, senior writer for The Gospel Coalition, reported that pastor suicides climbed 24 percent between 1999 and 2014.[12] This trend serves as further confirmation that the difficulties that accompany pastoral ministry only increase over time. It was anything but easy for the apostle Paul, and it is anything but easy for today's pastor. Atop your job description as a pastor is suffering. And if you serve a local body in this capacity for more than three weeks, it will become part of your résumé.

The apostle Paul's ministry, particularly as he outlined it in 2 Corinthians, is inspired proof that the pastorate is, in the words of Paul David Tripp, a dangerous, grueling calling. Dangerous, yes, grueling, sure, but glorious as well for the work it accomplishes both in and through God's ministers. The same apostle that wrote 2 Corinthians also penned, under the Spirit's inspiration, Romans 5:3–5: "We rejoice in our sufferings, knowing that suffering produces endurance, and endurance produces character, and character produces hope, and hope does not put us to shame."

TWO

JOHN CALVIN (1509-64): Faithful in Exile

W. ROBERT GODFREY AND JEFF ROBINSON

For many the name John Calvin evokes thoughts of a serious (even intimidating) theologian and a scholarly exegete of the Scriptures. Calvin was indeed those things, but for him theology and Bible study served his primary calling as a minister in the church of Jesus Christ. He was devoted to serving a local church in preaching and teaching, in visiting and counseling, in catechizing and disciplining as well as in writing.

Calvin did not come to the pastorate easily or automatically. As a student and young man, he was caught between three competing worlds. The first was the traditional French world of his father's influence and contacts. His father initially wanted him to have a career in the church and then switched to wanting John to study law. Even in the sixteenth century everyone knew that being a lawyer was the way to success. The second world, which interested John Calvin the most in his student years, was the world of Renaissance scholarship. Calvin wanted an academic life to study the work of ancient writers. His first published work was a learned study of the treatise "On Mercy" by the Roman Stoic philosopher Seneca.

The third world, to which Calvin was introduced through other students at university, was the world of the Reformation. Many students in Paris were drawn to Luther's efforts to reform the church. Calvin himself, after initial resistance, would in time embrace the Reformation.

The tensions among the worlds in which Calvin lived created a variety of struggles. He struggled with his sense of calling and with his religious convictions. When he accepted the teaching of the Reformation, he soon needed to flee from persecution in France. He still hoped for a scholarly life. His ability to write a clear and helpful introduction to Protestant theology not long after his conversion—his *Institutes of the Christian Religion* in 1536—demonstrated his remarkable talent as a thinker and a writer.

Calvin had planned to flee his native France for Strasbourg, in those days a quasi-independent city-state that was German speaking and part of the Holy Roman Empire. But he detoured to Geneva where he planned to pause briefly. Guillaume Farel, the initial reformer of Geneva, recognized that he needed a colleague with Calvin's learning and organizational skills to advance the reform there and threatened Calvin with God's judgment if he did not stay: "I denounce unto you, in the name of Almighty God, that if, under the pretext of prosecuting your studies, you refuse to labor with us in this work of the Lord, the Lord will curse you, as seeking yourself rather than Christ."[1] Farel's thundering voice was Calvin's call to the ministry. He found himself in exile with a calling he had neither sought nor wanted.

This first pastoral charge lasted less than two years. Calvin was young and uncompromising with a clear commitment to the freedom of the church to chart its own course and to practice its own discipline. He was also at times short-tempered, making submission to the authority of the city council—which governed the city-state of Geneva as well as the church there—difficult at times. When Calvin and Farel refused to administer the Lord's Supper at Easter in spring of 1538 because they had not been permitted to exercise discipline over some church members, the city council expelled them. In effect, Calvin continued his journey to Strasbourg but seemingly as an exile from pastoral ministry.

Calvin's plan was not God's plan.

In October 1538, Calvin wrote a letter from Strasbourg to his former congregation. Even in exile he showed no bitterness toward the council but reminded his former flock of the mysterious purposes of God—we do not always understand God's workings with us, but we can trust that his sovereign will is best. Calvin offers pastoral care in the form of counsel to consider how God might be at work in them through his ejection:

> You have besides to consider, that these things have not thus fallen out without the dispensation of the Lord, who carries forward his purposes even by means of the wicked, according to the good pleasure of his own will. Now, that thought will turn you away from the pursuit of your enemies, to consider and look into yourselves, and so to consider, that you may acknowledge that you may have well deserved on your part to receive such a visitation, to chastise your negligence, your

contempt, or even your careless slighting of the word of God. . . . Above all, take heed that you watch unto prayer; for if your whole expectation rests upon God, as it ought, there is good reason to infer that your heart should be daily lifted up to heaven. [2]

His life and the lives of those who supported the Reformation cause would be on the line from that time forward: "We have not only exile to fear, but that all the most cruel varieties of death are impending over us, for in the cause of religion they will set no bounds on their barbarity." [3]

Martin Bucer, the great reformer of Strasbourg, also recognized Calvin's talents and appointed him as pastor of a French refugee congregation there. Calvin learned a great deal from Bucer, especially about the worship and structure of the church. During his three years there, Calvin matured as a minister and accomplished a great deal. He wrote his first biblical commentary—on Romans; significantly expanded his *Institutes*; penned one of the greatest defenses of the Reformation, *A Reply to Sadoleto*; and also married. God was leveraging Calvin's exile to fashion the reformer into a pastor.

Back to Geneva

Then came the invitation to return to Geneva to take up his pastoral work there again. He did not want to go, seeing clearly that he would face continuing conflict and difficulty. Once again Farel had to intervene to persuade him. He returned in 1541 and served as minister there until his death in 1564. As he had feared, he experienced recurring serious troubles in several different arenas. His only child died in infancy, and his wife died relatively young, of which he writes to his close friend Pierre Viret: "I have been bereaved of the best companion of my life. . . . During her life she was the faithful helper of my ministry."[4]

A political faction that opposed him waxed and waned in influence, and at times Calvin feared he would be expelled again. He also feared the possibility of foreign attacks on the city. Only in the last decade of his life was the situation in Geneva peaceable. By then, however, his health was deteriorating, and he suffered from a variety of ailments ranging from kidney stones to a recurring fever.

In addition to his problems in Geneva, he also felt the pressure of the sufferings of his fellow Protestants throughout Europe. In his many letters he was often a counselor and encourager to those in trouble. Sometimes the pain was intense as when in June 1552 he had to write letters to five students from Geneva who had been imprisoned for their faith in Lyons and would ultimately be martyred for their faith. Calvin displayed his pastor's heart by pointing them to the One who would rescue them either by life or by death:

> We hope, come what may, that God of his goodness will give a happy issue to your captivity, so that we shall have reason to rejoice. You see to what he has called you; doubt not, therefore, that according as he employs you, he will give you strength to fulfill his work, for he has promised this, and we know by experience that he has never failed those who allow themselves to be governed by him.[5]

Through all of these trials and struggles, he remained frenetically active in preaching, teaching, and writing. On his deathbed, he was still dictating the last sections of his commentary on Joshua. Colleague and friend Theodore Beza urged him to rest, but Calvin responded: "What! Would you have the Lord find me idle?"[6]

Living in Exile

As a counselor Calvin was gentle and patient with the wavering while adamant and critical with the compromising. He stressed that Christians cannot engage in any acts of idolatry—especially attending Mass—to ensure their personal safety. They must be faithful and either suffer persecution or flee as exiles to a place of safety.

He gave that advice to Madame Bude, the widow of France's greatest humanist scholar, Guillaume Bude. Bude had had a religious outlook rather like that of Erasmus, but Madame Bude and her children had embraced Reformed Christianity. Calvin urged her to move to Geneva, but she found the decision for such a great change in her life difficult. In his letter of encouragement to her in 1546, Calvin used an arresting image. He writes, "For while we are in this world, it is fitting that we should be like birds upon the branch."[7] His point is that our attachment to our lives and their circumstances must be so slight that like birds on a branch we can easily flee away to wherever God would have us to be. God is in control, not us.

He also knew, however, that exile would not put an end to suffering, suffering that was ultimately governed by the hand of God. In 1549 he wrote a touching letter to Madame de la Roche-Posay, the abbess of a convent, pointing out that the primary cause of our trials is a loving God who is more concerned for our Christlikeness than for our comfort. He counsels:

I understand quite well, that in such bondage as you now are, you cannot serve God purely without the rage and cruelty of the wicked rising up immediately against you, and without the fire perhaps being lighted. . . . Howbeit, you must remember, that wherever we may go, the cross of Jesus Christ will follow us, even in the place where you may enjoy your ease and comforts. . . . For this is the very way whereby God would make trial of our faith, and know whether, in seeking after him, we have been renouncing self.[8]

Beyond faith in a general sense, Calvin looked to certain specific truths and promises of the Word of God—namely, his faith in Christ and his deep trust in God's providential will—to sustain him in his days of trouble. Calvin is famous for his strong teaching on the absolute sovereignty of God in daily providence and in predestination. For Calvin this doctrine is not abstract or speculative but intensely practical. As he powerfully expresses in his preface to his *Commentary on the Psalms*:

[The Psalms] will principally teach and train us to bear the cross. . . . By doing this, we renounce the guidance of our own affections and submit ourselves entirely to God, leaving him to govern us, and to dispose our life according to his will, so that the afflictions which are the bitterest and most severe to our nature, become sweet to us, because they proceed from him.[9]

As Christians our aim must be to grow in confidence in God's good purposes for us in all things so that we can embrace even our worst trials as coming from his fatherly and loving hand. Still, though God is sovereign, we don't always know his will for the future. We are called to depend on a sovereign God as pilgrims and strangers—exiles—in this world.

Calvin and a Pastoral Theology of Exile

Perhaps most fundamentally, Calvin was an exile whom God raised up to minister to exiles. Calvin was providentially displaced three times—from his home country in France, from Geneva to Strasbourg in 1538, and then back to Geneva in late summer of 1541.

A few days before his return from Strasbourg to Geneva, Calvin wrote to his intimate friend Guillaume Farel, admitting that his decision to return to the place at which he'd suffered the humiliation of expulsion was a path chosen by God, not one he would have chosen for himself. Farel had advised Calvin to return. Obviously, the reformer had needed some convincing:

> As to my intended course of proceeding, this is my present feeling: had I the choice at my own disposal, nothing would be less agreeable to me than to follow your advice. But when I remember that I am not my own, I offer up my heart, presented as a sacrifice to the Lord. . . . I submit my will and my affections, subdued and held-fast, to the obedience of God; and whenever I am at a loss for counsel of my own, I submit myself to those by whom I hope that the Lord will speak to me.[10]

From a human perspective, Calvin's original ouster made little spiritual sense. How would the church profit from so short a time with Calvin during his first tenure in Geneva? How would it now profit from his return? The answer to those questions took shape quickly as the exiled reformer became a minister to exiles. In ways unknown to us, God often prepares us well in advance to face challenges and perform his work in the future.

Beginning in 1542, Protestants from numerous regions and countries, including England, Italy, the Netherlands, Scotland, and Calvin's native France, fled to Geneva in a steady stream. All came seeking asylum from religious persecution in their home countries. Many, including scores of young men following a call to preach the Reformation's gospel of grace, came to Geneva because Calvin was there.

The population of Geneva doubled by 1555 and reached a peak of slightly more than twenty-one thousand by 1560. Having so many sympathizers to the Reformation cause gather in Geneva pleased Calvin: "I am . . . much preoccupied with the foreigners who daily pass this place in great numbers, or come here to live."[11] Ultimately, Calvin trained and prepared many of those refugees to return to their native lands as evangelists and pastors. Through Calvin's work, Geneva became a hub for foreign missions. Foremost on Calvin's heart was his homeland. Between 1555 and 1562, more than one hundred ministers left Geneva for France, clandestinely serving new churches there under threat of arrest and worse.[12]

The thrice-exiled Calvin teaches today's pastor at least four things related to a pastoral theology of exile.

Exile Is a Fundamental Posture for Every Minister

Calvin was a high-bred, brilliant man with clear gifts for writing; a bent toward close, careful study; and a personality seemingly more suited for the life of a scholar. Prior to being arrested by the wrathful threats of Farel, Calvin was en route to Strasbourg and a life of research and writing in service of the church. But God had other plans—Calvin served exactly half his life, twenty-seven years, as a pastor. To Calvin's mind, it was leaving a high calling to stoop down low—like Moses eschewing Egypt for the people of God or the Son of God forsaking the riches of heaven for the poverty of a fallen world.

As Calvin writes in commenting on 2 Corinthians 4:7, family trees and intellectual acumen are insignificant factors in God's economy:

> It is true, indeed, that all mortal men are earthen vessels. Hence, let the most eminent of them all be selected, and let him be one that is adorned to admiration with all ornaments of birth, intellect, and fortune, still, if he be a minister of the gospel, he will be a mean and merely earthen depository of an inestimable treasure.[13]

Exile Does Not Change the Pastor's Fundamental Calling of Faithfulness to God's Word

Calvin returned to Geneva on September 13, 1541. After being disgraced and ejected from his first pastorate there, surely Calvin would be tempted to unload on his opponents in his pulpit debut. In a 1540 letter, Calvin openly told Farel that he preferred to die "a hundred deaths to this cross" of returning to the church in Geneva.[14]

In his first appearance in the Geneva pulpit, Calvin responded in a far different manner than might be expected: he took up preaching the Bible at the chapter and verse at which he had left off forty months earlier:

When I came before the people to preach, everyone was eaten up with curiosity. But, remaining completely silent about the events which surely they all expected me to mention, I set forth very briefly the principles of my ministry, and then quickly and discreetly I recalled to mind the faith and the integrity of those who supported me. After this introduction I began to comment on the text at the place where I had stopped (at the time of my banishment). By doing this I wanted to show rather than having given up the teaching office, I had only been interrupted for a while.[15]

Exile Means Surrendering Our Desires, Personalities, and Gifts to God and Remaining Faithful When He Uses Them in Unexpected Ways

Calvin wanted to be a scholar. God wanted him to pastor in Geneva. God got his man. God's providence sometimes strikes us as strange because we are not writing our own script. This was certainly true in Calvin's story. The introverted Calvin preached God's Word faithfully at least a half-dozen times each week and faithfully shepherded his flock. He also wrote commentaries on most of the Bible, completed five editions of the *Institutes*, and published dozens of other theological works—all as a pastor. Calvin was the Reformation's pastor-theologian par excellence, though he never sought the first descriptor in that couplet. This in spite of a personality and gifts seemingly more bent toward academia. God used the necessity of reformation to reinvent Calvin the scholar as Calvin the pastor. In turn, God used him to raise up other pastors to shape and spread the Reformation's recovered gospel.[16]

Early biographer Jean-Daniel Benoit writes:

One loves to speak of him as the Reformer of Geneva. It would be perhaps more correct to refer to him as the pastor of Geneva, because Calvin was a pastor in his soul, and his reformatory work, in a good many respects, was only the consequence and extension of his pastoral activity.[17]

Calvin's life and ministry demonstrates that our desires, personalities, and gifts belong to God, and he often uses them in ways that we may never understand.

Exile Is God's Will, and His Meticulous Providence Will Comfort and Sustain Us When Perplexing Affliction Comes

Calvin sought to go to Strasbourg, and he finally got there by means of exile from Geneva—spirited there by the wicked decision of evil men. Calvin's stay in Strasbourg was brief, and his return to Geneva was unwelcomed. Pastors often face unjust suffering of various kinds from incorrigible critics inside the church to incomprehensible circumstances without. Even unjust suffering is not outside God's control, Calvin argues:

> When we are unjustly wounded by men, let us overlook their wickedness (which would but worsen our pain and sharpen our minds to revenge), remember to mount up to God, and learn to believe for certain that whatever our enemy has wickedly committed against us was permitted and sent by God's just dispensation.[18]

Conclusion

One contemporary teacher called the vocation of ministry a death sentence, meaning it is death to self-will and an embrace of God's will. When a man leaves safe harbor and guides his vessel into the tumultuous sea of pastoral ministry, he never knows which direction the waves may take him.

But, like Calvin, he can rest assured that God does know, and that truth liberates him to preach the gospel of grace with abandon, resting in Solomon's truth that while man makes his plans, a sovereign God orders his steps (Prov. 16:9).

THREE

JOHN BUNYAN (1628-88):
Faithful in Prison

TONY ROSE

Introducing you to John Bunyan in one chapter makes me smile. How do you describe in a few words a man who wrote sixty books? Thankfully, detailed descriptions of Bunyan's life are readily available elsewhere. I hope to give you a peek into his life that, like an appetizer, makes you want more.

I enjoy reading the life stories of great men from the past. I usually begin with great excitement. Excitement often leads to inspiration. But then, inspiration leads to discouragement. Why? Because I end up comparing the fruit of my ministry with theirs and fall quite short. Let me both explode that myth and confess my sin. When we read of how God used another in the work of the gospel it should always stir thankfulness in our hearts. Our discouragement over someone else's fruitful ministry reveals a selfish heart.

The benefit I now seek from reading about God's work through others is three-fold. First, few things teach and inspire me simultaneously like a good biography. It is like having a personal mentor from the past. Second, I am brought to confess my own sin. Such self-examination has become a light into the secret discontentment of my own soul. Finally, biographies can serve as a mirror into which I look to develop a more accurate self-understanding. Richard Baxter called it the benefit of self-acquaintance. Through the life of others, I more accurately learn my own gifts and capacities.

I offer a word of advice when reading about greats from the past. Our desire for heroes seems to produce an irresistible urge to dress up great saints of the past and make them a bit more attractive than they actually were. Our present need to inspire others can lead us to needlessly exaggerate and make our heroes into idols. But Bunyan stands out from the crowd of dead pastor-theologians. "The Tinker of Bedford" wrote his autobiography with such painful transparency that it is nearly impossible to make him more attractive than he actually was. Could we stand such transparency today?

Turbulent Life and Times

Writing to pastors about faithfulness amid suffering through the lens of Bunyan's life produced some serious confrontations in my soul. Truthfully, a normal day in Bunyan's life would be considered a day of great suffering for most of us. Bunyan's sixty years were lived during some of England's most turbulent times. England was filled with civil unrest. Deadly plagues and a bloody civil war left citizens staggering through life. The battles within civil leadership were paralleled by battles within the church.

Bunyan grew up in a small village about fifty miles north of London. He and his family were a bit distant from the political and ecclesiastical conflicts for a while. Bunyan's ancestors were landowners, but due to changing circumstances, by the time he was born the Bunyan clan was a rather poor lot. His dad was a tinker—that is, a brazier or tinsmith who made and repaired cooking pots and pans.

Bunyan had enough schooling to learn to read and write, but he was not well educated. Vocationally, he followed in his father's footsteps. We learn from Bunyan's *Grace Abounding to the Chief of Sinners* that he was a rather rascally youth. Because he was a natural leader, Bunyan was always first in the gang of neighborhood boys in their troublemaking escapades: "It was my delight to be taken captive by the devil [to do] his will. . . . From a child, I had but few equals . . . for cursing, swearing, lying, and blaspheming the holy name of God. So rooted and settled was I in these things, they became as a second nature to me."[1]

Bunyan's environment surrounded him with hardship. The Black Plague cast its grim shadow across England again when Bunyan was eight, killing more than thirty thousand people. Eight years later, his mother and sister both died within a month. His dad quickly remarried. At age seventeen, Bunyan joined Cromwell's Parliamentary army. He was among a group of soldiers selected for a dangerous mission to besiege a certain location. A fellow soldier asked to go in his place. A musket ball to the head killed Bunyan's substitute. Providence was guarding Bunyan for service in Christ's army.

Bunyan left the army in 1647 and began work as a tinker. England, however, remained in an uproar. Two years later, Charles I was put on trial and executed as a traitor. Bunyan married the same year. We don't know his first wife's name, but her Christian upbringing had considerable influence on him. Nine years into their marriage with four children younger than ten, one of whom was blind, his wife died. A year later Bunyan married Elizabeth. He was thirty-one; she was eighteen.

Pilgrim's Perilous Journey

Bunyan's interest in spiritual things seems to have been sparked by his first wife. Soon after their marriage, Bunyan began a process of serious outward transformations. People who knew him well were astonished at his newfound piety, but the changes were merely legalistic and external. One day while working, he overheard a group of women talking of spiritual things. He fancied himself rather good at spiritual conversation and joined them. Bunyan soon found himself out of his league. There was joy in their fellowship that he had never experienced. His heart yearned for what he saw in them. From that conversation Bunyan's spiritual journey began in earnest.

The Bible became the centerpiece of his life from that day till the day of his death. The unstoppable work of grace God began in Bunyan would lead him to the same joy in Christ those women had. But his path would be filled with torturous internal struggles that toggled between doubt and faith. He chronicled the journey with astounding frankness in his stunning spiritual autobiography, *Grace Abounding to the Chief of Sinners*.

Bunyan's path from conversion to assurance seems to have been his first phase of suffering. His intense internal battles enabled him to write with profound insight about the human experience. Battling through sins, doubts, an unsound mind, and the devil's onslaughts developed his assurance of God's love and produced strength of soul to faithfully suffer through twelve years in jail.

What Bunyan recorded of his experiences has proven difficult for some modern readers. Some see him as suffering from a severe mental malady. Others think his turmoil was strictly a spiritual experience in coming to a settled faith in Christ. After my thirty years of being a pastor and spending twenty-seven of those years living daily with the Puritans' works, I am convinced it was both. I am eternally grateful Bunyan chronicled his struggles. Had Bunyan not written of his personal battles on the way to finding strong assurance in Christ, I might still be as he once was—besieged by raging thoughts, up and down in assurance twenty times an hour.

Thankfully, those Christian ladies guided Bunyan to the church at which the godly Mr. Gifford was pastor. Bunyan's story is a beautiful picture of the local church being what God intended it to be. From the church at Bedford, Bunyan received pastoral care, biblical instruction, and Christian fellowship that led to a sound mind and a sound faith. *Grace Abounding* chronicles the parallel between his faith maturing and his mind becoming sound.

Preaching His Way into Jail

The Bedford church soon realized Bunyan was gifted to speak the gospel to the human heart. In the beginning of his ministry, he struggled with intrusive thoughts of the worst kind. Doubts still raised their heads and made him stumble. I think his every word was preached as much to himself as to his congregation. He was able to preach boldly even as strange thoughts and doubts welled up inside of him because he rested on the gospel that was outside of him.

The war between godly self-confidence and grueling self-doubt grew hottest in Bunyan when he climbed behind the sacred desk:

> Indeed, I have been as one sent to them from the dead; I went myself in chains to preach to them in chains; and carried that fire in my own conscience that I persuaded them to be aware of. I can truly say . . . when I have been to preach, I have gone full of guilt and terror even to the pulpit door, and there it hath been taken off, and I have been at liberty in my mind until I have done my work, and then immediately, even before I could get down the pulpit stairs, I have been as bad as I was before; yet God carried me on, but surely with a strong hand, for neither guilt or hell could take me off my work.[2]

Bunyan's fight to keep his faith in Christ alone is a model for pastors. Our weaknesses and temptations are reminders that our salvation and our ministry always depend on God, not us. An inkling of a thought that something in us helps guarantee our salvation or produces fruit in our ministry will lead us to either swell with foolish pride or get caught in the swift current of self-loathing.

The power of God's Spirit on Bunyan's preaching drew many people to hear him. He was becoming quite influential. Due to related governmental and ecclesiastical upheavals, church and state authorities told Bunyan he was not properly authorized to preach. He was ordered to stop or be jailed. Bunyan did not stop preaching the gospel. He knew God had called and commanded him to do so. He was arrested. Authorities attempted to get Bunyan to sign an agreement that he would no longer preach the gospel without the state church's authorization. If he did so, he could go free. Bunyan replied to their offer: "If I were out of prison today, I would preach the gospel again tomorrow by the help of God."[3]

Bunyan was found guilty and spent nearly thirteen years in jail. His suffering at times felt unbearable. He was deeply anguished over his young wife and the four children, especially daughter Mary who was blind: "I found myself a man, and compassed with infirmities; the parting with my wife and poor children hath oft been to me in this place as the pulling of flesh from my bones."[4]

Bunyan's wife pled eloquently to the magistrate for her husband's release, but even she was denied. Bunyan's life certainly seems like an odd process out of which to make an influential gospel preacher. But God does seem to use jails to prepare his finest servants.

Bridled Tongue, Unleashed Pen

What enabled Bunyan to stay faithful to God through such long and unjust suffering? One significant factor was his sense of spiritual responsibility. He had become a trusted leader. Many now looked to him for instruction and example. Bunyan knew that by signing the agreement he would not only dishonor God but also become a stumbling block to a multitude of suffering believers.

A few times Bunyan was given reprieve from jail, during which he would see his family and preach at every opportunity. He was always returned to jail, and the preacher's mouth would be shut. However, as has been the case since the prophets of the Old Testament, when the preacher is arrested his pen is set free.

Telling a preacher he cannot preach will either crush him or create him. God used the harshest of teachers to create a man of God out of the "chief of sinners." The faculty at Bunyan's school of internal suffering was composed of a few specialists—intrusive thoughts of a blasphemous nature that caused him to seriously think he had committed the unpardonable sin, unrelenting doubts about his salvation, and emotional upheavals that continually kept him haunted with fear. The devil used each of these issues to accuse and assault Bunyan at every turn:

> While I was in this temptation, I should often find my mind suddenly put upon it, to curse or swear, or to speak some grievous thing against God, or Christ his Son, and of the Scriptures. Now I thought, surely I am possessed of the devil.[5]

The faculty at Bunyan's school of outward suffering included poor living quarters in the jail, ongoing severe injustice, separation from family, and restraint from preaching.

There have been times while reading Bunyan I have felt fearful or nauseated and broke out in a nervous sweat. I sit stuck in my seat thinking, *Oh dear God, what would I do in such a situation? How did Bunyan see his way through?* At a point early in his long path to assurance in Christ, Bunyan said something like "From that day forward I was never out of my Bible." Bunyan's secret was no secret at all.

Through daily dependence on God's Word accompanied by the support of his church, he found sustenance to endure the unthinkable:

> I never knew what it was for God to stand by me at all turns, and at every offer of Satan to afflict me as I have found him since I came in [to jail]; for look how fears have presented themselves, so have supports and encouragements, yea, when I have started, even as it were at nothing else but my shadow, yet God, as being very tender of me, hath not suffered me to be molested, but would with one scripture and another strengthen me against all; I could pray for greater trouble, for the greater comfort's sake.[6]

Charles Spurgeon said of Bunyan that if you cut him he bled "bibline" because God's Word seemingly flowed through his veins. Though confined in jail Bunyan was not merely a self-absorbed reader of the Word. He intensely labored to translate the work of grace in his heart into written words for the spiritual benefit of others.

It may sound far too simple, but Bunyan remained faithful by keeping his mind on "the things that are above, where Christ is, seated at the right hand of God" (Col. 3:1) and by humbly counting others more significant than himself, looking "not only to his own interests, but also to the interests of others" (Phil. 2:4). Note that I said *simple*, not *easy*.

God's Word, not his circumstances, defined reality for Bunyan. Bunyan demonstrated that a mind set on Christ and serving his people produces a freedom no jail can confine. While in jail Bunyan wrote at least fourteen books and treatises, including *Pilgrim's Progress*. He left himself little time to think upon his suffering.

Lessons from Bunyan

Most of us will never suffer as Bunyan did. So how does his affliction help us today? The contrast between his life and ours is the key to one lesson from Bunyan. We can be blinded by admiration or envy of heroic men of God. We should not read them hoping to mimic their actions to produce similar results. God has given us the treasure of biographies so we can see the gospel at work deep inside his servants and learn to depend on Christ in our day as they did in theirs. Comparing the fruitfulness of our ministry with those of the past or with our contemporaries is an unhealthy exercise. Yet learning from the daily faithfulness of our brothers and sisters past and present is deeply beneficial.

A second lesson from Bunyan concerns a window he opened into his life that we often keep shut. I will call this closed window *secret sufferings*. These secret sufferings are acute in pastors (because many erroneously suppose we are stronger Christians than "mere" church members). Our skills at hiding them become sophisticated. We would feel no shame in talking about our physical sufferings. But how many of us would feel comfortable telling someone about our doubting mind? Would you tell anyone that before you went into the pulpit your mind at times was flooded with blasphemous thoughts and you feared you might actually say them out loud? Bunyan told the world such things in his autobiography. He opened the window on his secret sufferings to free others who were suffering in secret.

I think we would agree that Bunyan's journey to salvation and assurance is not a path common to all believers. In fact, Bunyan's description of his faith journey is so unusual to us that many Christians find him rather strange and his experience disturbing. He was a godly man, yet atheistic thoughts assaulted his mind and undermined his assurance:

> For about the space of a month . . . a very great storm came down on me, which handled me twenty times worse than all I had met with before; it came stealing upon me, now by one piece, then by another; first, all my comfort was taken from me, then darkness seized upon me, after which, whole floods of blasphemies, both against God, Christ, and the Scriptures, were poured upon my spirit, to my great confusion and astonishment. These blasphemous thoughts were such as also stirred up questions in me, against the very being of God, and of his only beloved Son; as, whether there were, in truth, a God, or Christ, or no? And whether the holy Scriptures were not rather a fable, and cunning story, than the holy and pure Word of God?[7]

Not everyone experiences the torturous processes of an obsessive mind like Bunyan. However, if we do—especially if we are pastors—we tend to keep that window closed. Doubts and blasphemous thoughts are considered off-limits for Christians, especially pastors.

Bunyan, like the young Martin Luther, had an overactive conscience and a faulty understanding of grace. This wedding of disparate spiritual partners left Bunyan open to forming terribly inaccurate conceptions of God and of himself. Wrong conceptions of God in an unsound mind can produce overwhelming floods of fear, depression, despair, and hopelessness.

On his worst days Bunyan could not tell the difference between the urges and impulses of his mind and emotions from the voice of God in Scripture. For instance, Bunyan said Satan perennially hammered him with questions about Scripture: "[Satan] would assault me with this, how can you tell but that the Turks [Muslims] had as good Scriptures to prove their Mahomet [Muhammad] the Saviour, as we have to prove our Jesus is?"[8]

Bunyan's experience is described in *Pilgrim's Progress* when Christian is walking through the valley of the shadow of death. Christian heard his thoughts as voices. He could not tell if his thoughts were his own or if someone else was speaking to him. Bunyan described how he would gain assurance from a Scripture passage suddenly coming to mind only to tumble into the pit of doubt by hearing a competing voice of accusation.

Free at Last

Reading *Grace Abounding to the Chief of Sinners* set me free. I was one of those pastors who experienced what Spurgeon called "fainting fits" and Richard Baxter called "a crazed wit." I kept my thoughts, feelings, and fears secret for years. The window to my soul was shut and locked. There was no way I would let anybody see inside me. I thought no one else, especially pastors, went through such things. I prolonged and intensified my secret suffering by keeping it hidden from others. Secrecy is the devil's tool. Bunyan's frightening transparency brought me comfort and gave me courage to open the window to my soul's dark corner. I learned from Bunyan that if I would ever know God and myself accurately, it must be through Scripture.

Our conceptions of God are worthless and dangerous unless they are formed by God's self-description in Scripture.

Without the gospel all our notions of God are mere carica-
tures. God made us in such a way that our true affections
follow our mind's impressions. That means to genuinely love
God we must know him truly. My ill concept of God mixed
with a subtle form of pride drove me to deep despair. I "felt"
I was such a terrible sinner that God could not forgive me.
My dear wife asked me one day, "Tony, what makes you
think you are so special that you are the only person in the
world God can't forgive?" It was the most stingingly insight-
ful question I had ever been asked.

With Bunyan's help I finally grasped the reality of my sinfulness and the necessity of resting on Christ's merits alone.
Stripped of all pretended righteousness, with all my sin exposed, God's gospel taught me to run to Christ. I no longer
needed "fig leaves"—closed windows to cover my unrelenting
shame. "Naked and exposed to the eyes of him to whom
we must give account," I heard the voice of Jesus, my High
Priest, say to me, "With confidence draw near to the throne
of grace" (Heb. 4:13, 16).

Resting completely on Christ, though confined to jail, John
Bunyan was no longer consumed with self but was set free
to get the gospel out to others. God used Bunyan's greatest
weakness to become his greatest strength. His obsessive mind
was now sanctified and unfettered to write unceasingly of
his majestic Savior.

Is it possible that you have a window to your soul you keep
shut? Are you ashamed to open it? Shame is a chain that keeps
us from the freeing power of God's grace. You may be trying
to hide the very part of you that God can greatly use. I leave
you with Bunyan's own words. If you need them I pray they
will help you, as they have me, to open that window and

exchange the chain of shame for the freedom of grace. They are summarized in the title of one of his works: *Come and Welcome to Jesus Christ*. In the school of affliction, Bunyan learned that Christ was his anchor amid the flood:

> Note, when providences are black and terrible to God's people, the Lord Jesus shows himself to them in wonderful manner; the which sometimes they can as little bear, as they can the things that were before terrible to them. They were afraid of the wind and water; they were also afraid of their Lord and Savior, when he appeared to them in that state. . . . Note, that the end of the appearing of the Lord Jesus unto his people, though the manner of his appearing be never so terrible, is to allay their fears and perplexities.[9]

FOUR

JONATHAN EDWARDS (1703-58): Faithful to the End

PETER BECK

The apostle Paul told the wayward congregation of Corinthians to do whatever they did to the glory of God
(1 Cor. 10:31). Jonathan Edwards told his congregation
the same thing from the beginning of his ministry among
them until the bitter end. He remained faithful to this grand
vision to the end of his life. In his posthumously published
The End for Which God Created the World, written while
in pastoral exile, Edwards observes, "All that is ever spoken
of in the Scripture as an ultimate end of God's works is
included in that one phrase, the glory of God."[1]

Jonathan Edwards stands as American evangelical Christianity's favorite son. He preached perhaps the most famous
sermon in the English language, "Sinners in the Hands of an
Angry God." He, along with George Whitefield and others,

embodied the power of the First Great Awakening. His fame extended to both sides of the Atlantic as his earliest works were published in hopes of preparing the church universal for a glorious work of God like the one in New England. Scholars today still laud him as America's greatest theologian and philosopher. To the unfamiliar or the barely familiar, Edwards represents the heights of God's work in early American history.

The rest of the story, however, is an American tragedy. It is the story of fame and infamy and of ecclesial disaster. Yet it is also the story of great faith in the God who works all things together for good (Rom. 8:28) and for his own glory (Rom. 11:36).

Destined for Greatness

> God is glorified in the wisdom of redemption in this, that there appears in it so absolute and universal a dependence of the redeemed on him.[2]

"Sinners" may be Edwards's most famous sermon, but it was far from his first famous sermon. "God Glorified in Man's Dependence," preached just two years into his pastoral ministry, presaged two decades of ever-increasing glory for the son of a preacher man. In fact, everything about Edwards and his call to the ministry foreshadowed greatness.

Though not famous, Edwards's father, Timothy, faithfully pastored his smallish congregation in East Windsor, Connecticut, for decades, modeling for his son the diligence necessary to complete the task before him. It was Edwards's grandfather, Solomon Stoddard, who enjoyed fame serving as the pastor of the most influential church in the farthest western reaches of Massachusetts. Well-known theological opponents such as the Mathers in Boston respected Stoddard and labeled him the "pope of the Connecticut valley," wittily criticizing his ecclesiological tendencies while acknowledging his profound reach. Unconcerned about accusations of nepotism or its potential consequences, Edwards accepted the call to join his grandfather in Northampton as his associate until Stoddard's six-decade ministry drew to a close. Edwards was anointed the heir apparent. Providence placed the young Edwards, just twenty-three years old, in the shadow and the way of greatness.

Less than three years later, in 1729, Stoddard "died in a good old age, an old man and full of years" (see Gen. 25:8). As Edwards climbed the stairs to the pulpit, his star was on the rise. All eyes would be on him to see to what heights the grandson of the great Solomon Stoddard would ascend. Within two years he would be preaching to the assembled ministers of Boston. They received his Election Day sermon, "God Glorified in Man's Dependence," with glad and appreciative ears. Upon their recommendation Edwards published the sermon, and his fame began to spread. Nothing compared, however, to the lofty accolades that followed in the middle years of that decade. In the fall of 1734, Pastor Edwards faithfully preached his way through a lengthy sermon series on the doctrine of justification by faith alone drawn from Romans 4:5: "And to the one who does not work but believes in him who justifies the ungodly, his faith is counted as righteousness." In the midst of that doctrine-heavy discourse, revival broke out in Northampton.

The quiet burg had experienced seasons of spiritual harvest several times under Stoddard, but they experienced nothing like what happened under Edwards. Over the next six months, the fires of revival spread from one home to another until nearly one-quarter of the population, upwards of three hundred of the town's twelve hundred residents, came under the saving influence of the Holy Spirit. News of the revival spread, and soon correspondents sought an account of the surprising work of God from the pastor in Northampton. With that account Edwards's renown spread farther—from New England to old England.

Though the excitement of 1734–35 died down less than a year later, God's grace revisited Northampton and the rest of the middle and northern colonies six years later. As the effect of the First Great Awakening grew, so did opposition. Cries of "we've never done it this way before" spread across New England. Once more Edwards was called upon, this time to defend the authenticity and the vitality of the Awakening. Edwards responded faithfully, and a number of works flowed from his pen to this end. Along with these defenses he engaged in a transatlantic dialogue on the nature of revival and calls for concerted prayer for revival. While Whitefield may be the most famous preacher of the Awakening, Edwards became the "theologian of revival," the man to whom his contemporaries and later generations would turn for an explanation of the glorious work of God in the conversion of the redeemed.

Destined for Failure

Edwards's prayer request to his pen pal, the Scotsman Thomas Gillespie, reveals the depths to which the mighty had fallen within a decade of the zenith of his fame during the First Great Awakening. Amid a great church conflict, Edwards writes:

> I desire your prayers that I may take notice of the frowns of heaven on me and this people (between whom was once so great an union), in the bringing to pass such a separation between us; and that these troubles may be sanctified to me; that God would overrule this event for his own glory (which doubtless many adversaries will rejoice and triumph in), that God would open a door for my future usefulness, and provide for me and my numerous family, and take a fatherly care of us in our present unsettled, uncertain circumstances, being cast on the wide world.[3]

Things had gone badly. Edwards went from the pastoral penthouse to the outhouse in less than ten years. The turn of events weighed heavily upon his heart. In hindsight, none of it surprised anyone.

Circumstances beyond his control conspired against Edwards and the hopes of a long, trouble-free tenure in Northampton, the first of which was his beloved grandfather, Solomon Stoddard. Edwards faced the daunting task of replacing the legacy pastor of a storied church. Stoddard served Northampton for nearly sixty years. He was the only pastor most in the town ever knew. Only death could separate him from the congregation he built and loved. For all his gifts and newfound stature, Edwards could never truly replace Stoddard in their hearts.

Circumstances, however, forced Edwards to try. As the flames of revival burned out, Edwards addressed the failure of the revival to change the spiritual and social tenor of the town. The seeming apostasy of so many recent converts required him to examine what had happened and to proffer solutions to correct their course once more. Edwards's most famous attempt, and perhaps the most lasting literary influence in his vast corpus, *Religious Affections* (1746), sought to defend the Awakening and promote Christian living among its converts by pointing out that many things masquerade as true conversion, including heightened emotions. True religious affections, however, show themselves in the believer's reveling in God's glory and bearing lasting fruit to that end. Edwards argued that not all professing believers are true believers—which likely included many among his congregation in Northampton.

The great treatise on the nature of saving faith proved insufficient to turn the tide of apathy in the church. With feigned agreement, they accepted his argument and denied its application. Thus, Edwards had to seek other ways to reform the assembled "saints" of Northampton. Like many modern-day pastors, Edwards sought to replace the current church covenant with one that reflected their current situation and addressed their spiritual needs, one in which the people were to "present [them]selves before the Lord, to renounce [their] evil ways, and put away [their] abominations from before God's eyes, and with one accord to renew [their] engagements to seek and serve God."[4] The congregation followed the lead of their pastor and accepted his recommendation. They endorsed the new covenant while ignoring its implications.

While most of the congregation embraced Edwards's idealism, many treated his attempts to reform the church as concerns for others but not for themselves. Such spiritual indifference ended up on the rocky shoals of Edwards's next "innovation."

Recognizing that many in their midst possessed little more than a cultural form of Christianity, Edwards wished to reclaim an insistence upon a believer's church akin to what he had studied in William Ames's *The Marrow Theology*, a text he was essentially required to memorize during his days at Yale. This novelty was not tested immediately. The church in Northampton languished through a spiritual drought that lasted six years before another person presented himself for membership. Upon Edwards's counsel a young man seeking admission into the church agreed to present his testimony before the congregation. The congregation balked. This insistence, they believed, violated the spirit of church membership instilled under the leadership of Stoddard decades earlier. Though long dead, their spiritual father still spoke (see Heb. 11:4). To prevent controversy, the young man withdrew his application. Later, a young woman presented herself for membership. Again controversy flared up, and again the church refused to hear Edwards's position. She was denied admission because she wasn't doing it the way they had in the past.

The presumed assault on Stoddard's legacy continued when Edwards wished to address admission to the communion table. Stoddard, against the wishes of his contemporaries such as Increase Mather, opened the Lord's Supper to not just local church members or even all believers but to all who desired to partake, including unbelievers. Stoddard was convinced that participation in the Lord's Supper might lead to the salvation of some. In the Supper, he reasoned, they saw and partook of God's grace in the crucifixion of Christ. In it, God might call them to salvation as they recognized their sinfulness and God's mercy. The Lord's Supper, he believed, is a "converting ordinance."

When initially called to Northampton, Edwards, a relative newcomer to the ministry and in awe of Stoddard's stature, accepted the practice of a truly open communion. Over time, however, he became convinced by Scripture that this was not biblical. He saw the spiritual stagnancy of the late 1740s as a reason to address the issue and correct their course. The people fell into open rebellion. They refused to listen to Edwards's explanation. They denied him the opportunity to use his pulpit to make his case. They forced his hand and made him put his ideas to paper. In the end, though, they also refused to read his treatise, *An Humble Inquiry*. They wanted nothing to do with his latest attempt to change their church.

Finally, the people of Northampton understood the implications of Edwards's ideas. By suggesting that a new church covenant was in order, Edwards was suggesting that the congregants, virtually everyone in town, failed to live up to their spiritual obligations. By requiring a valid profession of faith made in public, Edwards was suggesting their conversion and participation in the church may be invalid. By restricting the unbeliever's access to the Lord's Supper, Edwards might restrict their participation in an ordinance that many believed to be their birthright, the right of all who had been baptized upon birth rather than the new birth. Edwards's ideas, they knew, assaulted more than Stoddard's spiritual legacy. It undermined theirs.

Destined for Glory

I need the prayers of my fathers and brethren who are friendly to me, that I may have wisdom given me by my great master, and that I may be enabled to conduct with a steady faithfulness to him, under all trials and whatever may be the issue of this affair.[5]

With the embers of the Awakening long dead and the fire of controversy in full flame, Edwards cast his future on the will of God; he called on friends near and far to pray on his behalf. With no resolution in sight and no hope for an amicable solution, the church and their pastor agreed to allow a council to convene, a committee to decide his fate. As they had done concerning the publication of Edwards's views on communion, he and the church negotiated the details of this conclave, each hoping to their own advantage. Edwards mistook the compromise as a hopeful sign of God's providence.

Edwards and the church determined that each side in the dispute would be represented by an equal number of hand-chosen friends or emissaries. Representing the church were friends and relatives of Solomon Stoddard, avowed enemies of the arrogant grandson who besmirched his memory. Representing Edwards would be friends and disciples from across the region. When the conclave gathered, June 19–22, 1750, the storm clouds had gathered but not all of Edwards's representatives had. Worse, when surveyed on behalf of the council, only 10 percent of the congregation desired to retain Edwards as pastor. Then with a final, fateful vote, the council concluded the most famous pastor in American church history should be removed from his congregation. In the end Edwards lost the confidence of his people, and he lost his church by one vote. Yet Edwards's faith remained unshaken. As one witness remembered, "I never saw the least symptoms of displeasure in his countenance the whole week, but he appeared like a man of God, whose happiness was out of reach of his enemies."[6]

Farewell, but Faithful

Weeks later, Edwards preached what John Piper believes to be "one of the most remarkable sermons that he—or perhaps any other pastor—has ever preached."[7] Edwards fittingly drew his "Farewell Sermon" from 2 Corinthians 1:14: "Just as you did partially understand us—that on the day of our Lord Jesus you will boast of us as we will boast of you." Speaking of one final, future gathering of this pastor and his congregation, Edwards spoke of the coming judgment at which both he and they would stand before Christ and give an account of their relations with him and with one another. While painfully forthright with his audience about their complicity in the preceding controversy, he acknowledged his own shortcomings. Moreover, he spoke tenderly of his concern for their eternal well-being, offering both his heart and his prayers on their behalf. As he concluded, "But now I must bid you farewell. I must leave you in the hands of God: I can do no more for you than to pray for you."[8]

Edwards rightly knew this last appearance before his former congregation would not be his last, but he wrongly assumed their next meeting would be in eternity. Their meetings would be much sooner and much more frequent. With nowhere else to go, Edwards and his family remained in Northampton while they waited for God's will to become apparent. As awkward as that must have been for him—there was only one church in town for him and his family to attend—the church begrudgingly came back to Edwards and asked him to fill his former pulpit until they could find a suitable replacement. Edwards supplied the pulpit for months before finally admitting the burden was unhealthy for them. A contingent of parishioners approached Edwards vowing their support should he decide to start a second church in Northampton. He graciously acknowledged their loyalty but demurred on account of his desire to be no further burden to his old congregation.

Thus, after nearly twenty-five years in Northampton, Edwards found himself cast upon turbulent seas with no prospect of security in sight. His faith, however, remained intact. He tells one correspondent, "I have now nothing visible to depend upon for my future usefulness, or the subsistence of my numerous family. But I hope we have an all-sufficient, faithful, covenant God to depend upon. I desire that I may ever submit to him, walk humbly before him, and put my trust wholly in him."[9]

Edwards's tale of faithfulness does not end in failure, however. In what might be considered his wilderness experience as he literally proceeded into the wilderness of Massachusetts to serve as pastor of a small missionary outpost that ministered to the native population, Edwards served the church at large in a way heretofore impossible. Though God did not directly answer Edwards's many prayers during the controversy, he answered a greater kingdom need. Free of the hassles of an unappreciative congregation, Edwards produced many of his greatest and most important works during his five-year sojourn in Stockbridge. He wrote *Freedom of the Will*, *Original Sin*, and his two treatises, *The Nature of True Virtue* and *The End for Which God Created the World*. These works continue to affect Christians and have secured Edwards's legacy for generations to come.

Years later, worried about unfinished works, Edwards reluctantly accepted the call to the presidency of the College of New Jersey (Princeton) on the advice of friends who believed God had greater plans yet. After his arrival, in an attempt to lead the local population by example, Edwards received an immunization against small pox, a common killer in early America. Unfortunately, he contracted the disease and died within weeks. To the end Edwards remained faithful to God and his will for his life.

Faithful Example

By all appearances Edwards was destined for greatness. He enjoyed opportunities many pastors long for. Edwards had the right family name. The most famous preacher of the day hired him to be his associate, heir to a most important pulpit. After just one sermon he became famous, a published author. His preaching led to revival, a significant renewal of a long-established church. After that revival, he became a noted expert, his opinion on a host of matters sought after by those who recognized his genius. His writings influenced pastors across the English-speaking world. Change the name and the context and Jonathan Edwards's story represents the aspirations and hopes of many pastors of our generation.

Yet Edwards's greatest example may be what we find in his failure. He proves that pedigree guarantees nothing, neither success nor appreciation. If the greatest theologian in American history can be removed from his pulpit for standing on principle, it can happen to anyone. Edwards's example teaches the powerful lesson that one's legacy is not built upon popularity, or lack thereof, but on faithfulness to God and a willingness to be used as God sees fit, whether in fame and fortune or anonymity and sacrifice.

Had Edwards not been fired, some of the most important theological works in the last 250 years might not have been written. Setting his reputation aside, consider the fact that *Freedom of the Will*, written after his dismissal while he labored among the Indians of Stockbridge, became the theological foundation that would help launch the modern missionary movement in England forty years later. Likewise, it was not Edwards's pastoral ministry that shaped evangelicalism in the nineteenth century but his *Religious Affections* and *The Life of David Brainerd*. Today Edwards's legacy is not measured by his failures but by his faithfulness.

FIVE

JOHN NEWTON (1725–1807): Faithful amid Disappointment

TOM SCHWANDA

In 1763 John Newton wrote to his friend, Thomas Haweis, and declared that if he were ever ordained, the essential foundation for his ministry would be "Grace, free Grace must be the substance of my discourse—to tell the world from my own experience that there is mercy . . . for the most hardened."[1] Many readers will know the basic outline of Newton's life and how deeply he needed the free grace of God. His mother died of tuberculous before he was seven. Newton joined his father at sea when he was eleven, thus suppressing the early religious training of his mother. Numerous voyages on slave-trading vessels created a hardened heart that revealed gross immorality and wickedness. Newton prided himself in leading others into similar temptations and gross blasphemy. His efforts to profit from slave trading misfired, and instead he was imprisoned and brutally treated worse than a slave.

Later while crossing the Atlantic, a violent storm threatened to destroy his vessel and brought him to his knees, crying out for God's mercy. At this same time, Newton had casually begun reading Thomas à Kempis's devotional classic, *The Imitation of Christ*, and had experienced some stirrings in his neglected conscience. Miraculously, the ship reached the safety of land. Newton dated this March 21, 1748, event as his conversion but soon realized he was not a true believer until six months later.

He continued slave trading for many years until a seizure finally ended his sailing career in 1754. This might raise questions regarding the validity of his conversion, but at this period evangelicals did not yet see slavery as a vile sin. With increasing maturity, Newton lamented his former occupation and wrote a tract condemning slavery in 1787. Through his friendship with William Wilberforce, Newton encouraged his abolitionist efforts in Parliament.

Amid his numerous voyages, in 1750 Newton married Mary Catlett, better known as Polly. He found work as a tide surveyor in Liverpool and was responsible for inspecting cargo and preventing smuggled goods. Shortly before he started his civil service he met George Whitefield. A few years later he met John Wesley. As early as 1757 Newton began wrestling with whether he was being called to an ordained ministry.

Trials in Seeking Ordination

This was the beginning of seven years of intense frustration, inner struggle, and frequent questioning as Newton sought ordination in the Church of England. Numerous hurdles confronted him along the way. Many who lacked his determination would have given up long before he reached his coveted dream. For example, he lacked the proper credentials of a university education required of Anglican clergy. Exceptions were made for those who demonstrated a strong knowledge of Scripture and theology. Newton had taught himself Greek and Hebrew and had read widely in theology. Apparently the real reason for his rejection was his association with Methodists. In the eighteenth century, the term *Methodist* referred to any person who was "awakened" or born again to new life in Christ. Critics often accused Methodists of "enthusiasm." Today, ministers encourage a sincere and passionate response to the gospel. But in Newton's day, the term *enthusiasm* described people who were excessive in their spiritual practices, ministered outside of the Church of England, and stressed the necessity of evangelical conversion. In the previous century, enthusiasm also described people on the fringe who sought to overthrow the government.

While Newton was stunned by his initial defeats, he persisted for seven years in his desire for ordination. When prospects within the Church of England repeatedly failed, Newton questioned whether to accept any of the numerous invitations he had received from Independent and Presbyterian churches. John Wesley also invited him to become an itinerant minister with his expanding movement. Polly and her family strongly discouraged Newton from any consideration of non-Anglican ministry. This was based primarily on financial and social reasons, not spiritual ones.

Some of his relatives were shocked that he would consider leaving his lucrative government position for the instability and meager income of ministry. We can hear the deep determination and strong desire to surrender to God in a letter written to a friend in 1762: "As to laying aside all thoughts of the Ministry, it is quite out of my power: I cannot, I will not give up the desire; though I hope I shall not run before I am sent."[2] Newton's sensitivity to God's greater wisdom and timing is quite remarkable considering all his rejections.

His persistence was finally rewarded when he was ordained an Anglican minister in 1764. By that time he had presented his request to at least two bishops, two archbishops, and even the archbishop of Canterbury. The difference this time was that Thomas Haweis introduced Newton to the powerful and evangelical Lord Dartmouth. Through his influence Newton was granted the necessary meeting to be examined for ordination.

Newton's Pastoral Ministry

Lord Dartmouth was also instrumental in sending Newton to Olney, where he served until 1779. From there he moved to St. Mary Woolnoth in London, where he ministered until his death in 1807. Newton developed a friendship with William Cowper during his time at Olney. By 1773 Cowper fell into deepening depression and attempted suicide numerous times. Despite his frequent battles with mental health, Cowper contributed about 20 percent of the hymns to the famous *Olney Hymns* (1779). This contained Newton's "Amazing Grace" as well as other hymns still popular today: "How Sweet the Name of Jesus Sounds," "Glorious Things of Thee are Spoken," and others.

Early in his ministry, Newton discovered the financial challenges of serving in the church. While he was appointed the minister in charge at Olney, the previous minister still occupied a nominal position and received one-third of Newton's salary. Newton was no stranger to an assortment of trials and challenges that have plagued ministers from the earliest times. A nearby minister gave him a hostile greeting that shocked Newton. This antagonism was due most likely to his association with Methodists. Fortunately his reception among his new congregation was more cordial. However, during the early stages of the American Revolution, Newton made comments that some critics interpreted as supporting the American colonists rather than his own homeland. Taken together, Newton experienced numerous trials during his first ministry: jealousy from other ministers, meager financial support, stress of supporting an emotionally unstable church member, and political attacks.

Newton's move to London created increased opportunities to influence the evangelical cause. He became the most prominent evangelical Anglican in England. He either found or assisted in the formation of the Eclectic Society—a group of notable evangelical ministers and laity with an emphasis on missions that would merge into the Church Missionary Society—and the British Foreign Bible Society.

Newton's many years of personal struggle both before and after his ordination prepared him for a significant ministry of correspondence. Through his letters, Newton provided spiritual direction to numerous clergy and laity. His moderate Calvinism shaped an irenic attitude that appropriated a wide theological spectrum, including his favorable reception of Roman Catholic authors such as Fénelon and Pascal.

Survival Skills during His Struggle for Ordination

There were four primary reasons Newton was able to withstand his unrelenting struggles over a seven-year period.

First, Newton was renewed by a constant reminder that he believed he had truly been called by God to gospel ministry. This conviction had been confirmed during an intense six-week process in which Newton carefully journaled and examined his heart to test whether he was spiritually mature and ready for ordination. He named this work *Miscellaneous Thoughts and Enquiries Upon an Important Subject* and engaged in Bible study, meditation, prayer, and fasting. He used Paul's epistles to Timothy and Titus, John 14–17, and 1 John to examine his motivations for ministry. This intense period of self-examination also included wrestling with which denomination he should serve if ordained. Despite his manifest unworthiness, which he quickly confessed, Newton reached a decision in 1758 on his thirty-third birthday: God had called him to the ministry.

Second, Newton placed his total confidence in God. This was more than a cliché; it was a deep conviction that sustained him amid the varied defeats faced in coming years. One of the most critical factors for any Christian—especially ministers—is how a person perceives God. This is more than articulating a proper theological definition to defend one's orthodoxy but the inner heart perceptions that reveal most clearly how a person actually understands God. Significantly, this inner perception exerts more influence in one's relationship with God and others than the theologically correct confession a person might speak. Newton clearly affirmed God's sovereignty, no doubt learned from his earlier struggles and suffering. He was amazed that God had preserved his life through myriad dangerous voyages at sea. He learned the lesson of waiting even in the uncertainty of time. Once again this response demonstrates God's amazing grace that supported and sustained him through trials.

Third, Newton had the right perspective on affliction. It is common for contemporary Christians to see trials and challenges as a sign of God's displeasure or even punishment. Not so for Newton. Among the most enduring legacies of Newton are his precious letters of spiritual counsel. Early in his ministry these epistles were highly acclaimed for their wisdom, depth of pastoral sensitivity, and biblical promises. Paging through the volumes of his letters one recognizes a sampling of his understanding of affliction. According to Newton, suffering helps a person better grasp the meaning of Scripture and experience the sweetness of God's promises, strengthens a person's fellowship with God, weakens the effect of indwelling sin, and weans a person from the deceptive enticements of the world. In other words, it prepares one for heaven.

Newton was quick to add that trials and afflictions are never random but are personalized for each individual to produce the desired results of sanctification and maturity in Christ. That is why the proper response is not resentment or flight but submission to trials, since they come from a loving God. Newton writes of this in the final verse of his hymn, "I Asked the Lord That I Might Grow":

> These inward trials I employ
> From self and pride to set you free,
> And break the schemes of earthly joy
> That thou may'st find your all in me.[3]

One text Newton frequently referenced when addressing affliction was 2 Corinthians 12:9–10:

> But he said to me, "My grace is sufficient for you, for my power is made perfect in weakness." Therefore I will boast all the more gladly of my weaknesses, so that the power of Christ may rest upon me. For the sake of Christ, then, I am content with weaknesses, insults, hardships, persecutions, and calamities. For when I am weak, then I am strong.

"My grace is sufficient" in many ways represents the motto for Newton's life and ministry. The importance of this phrase is reflected in one of his hymns, "My Grace Is Sufficient for Thee." And further, in a variation of Romans 8:28, Newton taught, "All shall work together for good: everything is needful that *he sends*; nothing can be needful that *he withholds*."[4] Newton communicated the same liberating truth in his hymn "Be Gone, Unbelief, My Savior Is Near," in which the first verse ends: "With Christ in the vessel, I smile at the storm."

Fourth, Newton was always surrounded by a supportive community. He cultivated friendships with ease and formed a wide network across diverse boundaries. For example, members of the Eclectic Society included Independent, Methodist, and Moravian pastors and laymen. He was not afraid to bare his soul and honestly confess his doubts and fears. His vulnerability produced sensitive friendships that would give him a clear perspective.

When Newton was presented with possible opportunities, he was quick to seek the guidance of trusted friends. He understood that emotions have the potential to distort reality and radically alter a person's judgment. But the most significant relationship in his life was with Polly. Unlike some other early evangelical leaders whose marriages were a disaster, John loved Polly, and they enjoyed each other. Polly's health was always frail, and eventually she suffered through a long and debilitating battle with cancer that took her life in 1790. Newton spoke of his loss of Polly as "my great trial."

Contemporary Trials

Before I became a professor, I served as a pastor for three churches over eighteen years. In one of those congregations I was an associate pastor. When the head pastor retired, the church called a new senior pastor in just two weeks. This alarmed most of the congregation, since in my tradition the church typically spends at least one year in a careful self-study to determine the needs of the church and expectations of the new leader.

No sooner did the pastor arrive when he announced his plans to terminate the entire church staff. That meant all of the pastors and other staff members lost their positions in a few months. Suddenly I lost my ministry. I struggled for months asking, Why? What is next? How do I survive the lack of income? Like Newton, I too experienced God's faithfulness in providing—even though it wasn't on my timetable.

Through this extremely painful valley of darkness from which it took many years to emerge, I learned three lessons that kept me sane.

First, like Newton I recognized the value of supportive friends with whom I could be honest. Unlike some Christians who seek to create a polished veneer without struggles, my wife and I were intentional to be appropriately vulnerable and reveal our pain and brokenness. I discovered that many pastors and church leaders had been dismissed from their ministries for no valid reason other than manipulation or abuse of power. Second, like Newton I continued my previous habits of journaling and meditating on Scripture. It is common when people suffer trials or afflictions to discontinue spiritual practices, believing God doesn't care or has forgotten them. In addition to my regular Bible reading, I began praying the Psalms daily. I read them slowly in a meditative fashion and would often return to the same passage the next day. This practice cultivated a richer language for prayer, including the frequent reminder of the psalms of lament that invite those who struggle to cry out to our Triune God for help. Laments are based on the premise that while the believer struggles, God responds to our cries of affliction with love and in power. This also taught me to see more clearly the awesome nature and character of God.

Third, like Newton I learned the value of gratitude. Whether simple or more profound, I recorded my thankfulness for people, experiences, and insights. Gratitude had the surprising benefit of expanding my myopic vision beyond my own limited pain to see more fully. I discovered many people who suffered physically, spiritually, mentally, or relationally. I could intercede for them even as others were praying for me.

Ministry Insights

Newton reminds us that pastoral struggles and doubts are not infrequent or unusual but the norm. In fact, if we are not experiencing some sort of pastoral tension or conflict, it may well mean we are not attempting anything challenging to encourage the growth of the people we serve. When—not if—problems surface, it is not uncommon to second-guess our decisions or the particular aspect of ministry that either caused or resulted from the trials. But ministers should not read these as signs of God's absence or neglect but as potential confirmation that we are doing something right.

Newton teaches us the critical value of trust in our sovereign God, realizing his providence is just as active in this day as in Newton's day. This confidence comes from both a commitment to cultivate a vibrant spiritual maturity and a trust in God's steadfast love and faithfulness. If we believe our convictions are biblical, we should seek to be faithful to God, even if it results in conflict or sharp criticism from others.

Newton also instructs us in the importance of patience and careful deliberation. When feeling trapped in a difficult or painful ministry, some believe the best way out is to jump at the first opportunity that arises and flee. Too many pastors spend a few years in a ministry only to search for a larger, wealthier congregation. This can be dangerous for many reasons. It is difficult for pastors or missionaries to create a healthy ministry if they don't spend enough time getting to know and trust the people they serve and vice versa. Newton served only two churches; both were long-term ministries. As indicated earlier, Newton sought the wisdom of trusted friends who could see a difficult situation more objectively than he could. And further, Newton was sensitive not to run ahead of God's timing before he was actually sent.

Amazing Grace

It can be dangerous to critique a person from the distance of history because we don't know all the details. And even for one as prolific as Newton in his diaries, his writing does not reveal everything. For example, some readers might disagree with Newton's patience with Polly in not accepting numerous opportunities extended to him outside the Church of England. He chose to wait until she was ready and depended on her approval in his decisions. While some might question his approach, I see it more as an indication of his wisdom. He was sensitive enough to realize that in healthy marriages spouses must listen and wait and not force their partners into something before they are ready.

Newton had learned humility through his struggles in his slave-trading years, which was further refined throughout his ministry. In 1779 Newton's most famous work was published, a hymn that has come to be one of the most famous songs in history—in and outside of the church. It well summarizes the grace every minister needs to run the race of faith with endurance: "Through many dangers, toils, and snares I have already come. . . . He will my shield and portion be as long as life endures."[5]

SIX

ANDREW FULLER (1754–1815): Faithful amid Heartbreak

STEVE WEAVER

Although Andrew Fuller is a long-neglected figure, studies about him are enjoying a renaissance.[1] William Carey, the father of modern missions, has understandably received much more interest academically and popularly. Lesser known is the circle of friends who served with Carey to awaken the English Baptists of the late eighteenth century to the cause of global missions.

Chief among these friends was Andrew Fuller, a pastor-theologian who was one of the most prominent polemicists among evangelicals at the turn of the nineteenth century. Fuller, whom Charles Spurgeon called "the greatest theologian of the century,"[2] was unquestionably the theologian behind the modern missionary movement. Yet even among those who have become acquainted with his theology, few know Fuller's faithfulness throughout a lifetime of heartbreak.

Who Was Andrew Fuller?

Andrew Fuller was born on February 5, 1754, in the village of Wicken in Cambridgeshire, England. He was born into a family of Baptists at a time when the Particular Baptists of England were strongly influenced by what is known as hyper- or high-Calvinism. *Hyper-Calvinism* is a term used to refer not to those who merely believe in the five points of Calvinism but to those who additionally affirm the eternal justification of the elect and reject the public and promiscuous proclamation of the gospel. The doctrine of eternal justification was sometimes used as an excuse not to openly invite all people to believe the gospel.

Instead, hyper-Calvinists believe that one should wait for a "warrant" or evidence of election in individuals before calling sinners to believe in Christ. Although the evangelical revival was flourishing in the United Kingdom through the preaching of men such as John Wesley and George Whitefield, most Particular Baptist congregations remained unaffected by this evangelistic movement.

Fuller's own personal testimony is the story of his times in miniature. He was raised in a hyper-Calvinistic background. His own pastor rarely addressed unbelievers. His early experience led to later questions regarding the sinner's duty to believe in Christ. The teaching that evidence of election was necessary before the opportunity to believe the gospel could be set before any sinner led Fuller to languish for a number of years without the confidence to approach Christ for mercy. Although Fuller read John Bunyan's *Pilgrim's Progress* and many other works that told of Christ's sufficiency to save, he still lacked confidence that he had the right to believe in Christ.

Eventually Fuller found what he was so desperately seeking in the Word of God. Divine warnings and promises together drove Fuller to faith in Christ. In 1770 Fuller was baptized and became a member of the local Baptist church in Soham. Five years later he became that church's pastor. However, in his early years as pastor, he was still influenced by the hyper-Calvinism of his youth and did not dare invite the unconverted to come to Jesus. By 1778 all that had changed. Fuller's study of Scripture, his rereading of Bunyan, and his fellowship with pastors John Sutcliff of Olney, John Ryland Jr. of Northampton, and Robert Hall Sr. of Arnesby led him to change his view. Hall had introduced Fuller to the writings of the American theologian Jonathan Edwards, specifically recommending his treatise on the freedom of the will.[3]

Edwards's distinction between moral and natural ability/ inability was seized upon by Fuller as a way of understanding both how sinners have the duty to respond to the preaching of the gospel and why Christians have the responsibility to offer the gospel to all indiscriminately. In 1781 Fuller wrote a book that would become one of the main theological foundations for the modern missionary movement. The title of the book nearly says it all: *The Gospel of Christ Worthy of All Acceptation: or The Obligations of Men Fully to Credit, and Cordially to Approve, Whatever God Makes Known. Wherein is Considered the Nature of Faith in Christ, and the Duty of Those Where the Gospel Comes in That Matter.*[4] It is commonly known simply as *The Gospel Worthy of All Acceptation*, and it strongly called for the "promiscuous" proclamation of the gospel to all peoples.

Fuller's commitment to world missions was shown not only in his writings but also in his actions. He was instrumental in the formation of the Baptist Missionary Society in 1792, which sent out his friend William Carey, "the father of modern missions," to India. Fuller was elected the first secretary of the society and kept that position until his death by tuberculosis on May 7, 1815.

Trials of Andrew Fuller

Throughout his ministry, Fuller experienced his share of physical and emotional suffering. Specifically, he had a stroke in 1793 that resulted in headaches for the rest of his life. He also seems to have been prone to a depression that plagued him intermittently throughout his life. In addition, Fuller dealt with what the apostle Paul calls "the daily pressure . . . of . . . anxiety for all the churches" (2 Cor. 11:28). By all accounts Fuller was a faithful pastor, father, and husband. His faithfulness to his pastoral, familial, and missional responsibilities even while enduring heartbreaking trials with dear family members is the focus of the remainder of this chapter.

Heartbreak of the Loss of a Child

Fuller experienced the loss of eight children. In an era of high childhood mortality, most of these were lost in infancy. However, two of his children from his first marriage, Robert (whose story will be explored below) and Sally, survived infancy, and both were the source of terrible heartbreak for their father. In a journal entry from December 1785, Fuller speaks of his ill little girl and confesses, "If God should take either of my children from me, I seem as if I could scarcely sustain it."[5]

Over the next several months, Fuller's diary was filled with references to his fears about the health of his six-year-old daughter. On January 8, 1786, Fuller writes, "Exceedingly distressed . . . I fear God will take away my child."[6] Fuller struggled with whether he was being chastised by God. Concern for his little girl occupied his mind at all times. On February 5, he writes that "the measles came out" on Sally. Of the period from March 12 to April 16, Fuller writes that he "had great exercise of heart, on account of my poor little daughter: sometimes, pleading hard with God, on her account; at other times, ready to despair, fearing that God would never hear me." On April 21, he admits that "if God were to cut off my poor child, and were not to afford me some extraordinary support under the stroke, that I should be next to dead to the whole creation, and all creation dead to me!" Six days later he writes that he was "willing to leave her in the hands of God." And on May 7, Fuller writes:

> I was tolerably supported under the approaching death of my poor child, which I saw drawing on apace. I saw I must shortly let her fall. With floods of tears, with all the bitterness of an afflicted father mourning for his firstborn, I committed her to God, to his everlasting arms when she should fall from mine.

Nevertheless, the blow would not be easy. Fuller's entry for the period of May 14 to 31 began bleakly. "Death! Death is all around me!"[7] On May 25, he was especially overwhelmed with grief. He "lay before the Lord, weeping like David, and refusing to be comforted." His grief was so great that he became ill and was unable to see his daughter in her final days. He describes how he learned of her passing from his own sick bed:

> On Tuesday morning, May 30, as I lay ill in bed, in another room, I heard a whispering. I inquired, and all were silent . . . all were silent! . . . But all is well! I feel reconciled to God. I called my family round my bed. I sat up, and prayed as well as I could; I bowed my head, and worshipped, and blessed a taking as well as a giving God.

Two days later Fuller was able to get up and attend his daughter's funeral preached by his friend John Ryland Jr. from 2 Kings 4:26—"It is well." Fuller stated that he felt "in general now, a degree of calm resignation." A few days later, he would record that his "resignation and serenity" came due to his belief that "the event was decided by an infallible God."[8] He hoped not in the belief that God had nothing to do with his daughter's death. Rather, he found comfort in trusting a sovereign God who cannot err. In a meditation on the "Mystery of Providence" from Job 12:6–25, Fuller declares that "it is a part of that great system of providence that directs all human suffering, and will ultimately issue in the greatest good."[9] Fuller's confidence in God's sovereignty enabled him to see, even through tears, that his heartbreak would result finally in his good and God's glory.

On June 3 he stood over her grave "with a great deal of composure" and "felt a sort of triumph over death." The next day he preached on "these light afflictions" with a "calm and serene" mind.[10] Although not necessarily the same sermon referenced, Fuller once preached a sermon on "The Magnitude of the Heavenly Inheritance" from Romans 8:18–23 in which he described how heavy afflictions could be considered light. He preached to others in words that he surely had to preach to himself: "They may be heavy and tedious, when viewed by themselves; but weighed against a far more exceeding and eternal weight of glory, they are light and momentary."[11] It was Fuller's confidence in the future reward and reunion of heaven that enabled him to endure the heartbreak of the loss of a child.

Heartbreak of the Loss of a Wife

Another source of heartbreak was the loss of his first wife, Sarah. This occurred in August 1792, although for three months prior she seemed to have suffered from a form of dementia or Alzheimer's. As anyone who has faced this hardship within their family or with a church member can attest, this is a dreadful disease. Alzheimer's has often been called "the long good-bye." On July 10, 1792, Fuller writes in his diary, "My family afflictions almost overwhelmed me; and what is yet before me I know not! For about a month past, the affliction of my dear companion has been extremely heavy."[12] The day before, he had written in more detail in a letter to his friend John Ryland:

> My domestic trials are exceedingly great, far, very far, beyond what I ever met with before. I was taken ill last Friday, July 7, with a pain under my left breast, and was bled on Saturday. Yesterday, (Lord's Day), I could not engage in any thing, nor could I have done so, if Mr. Hall, who providentially was in town, had not been here. I feel better this morning, though I have had but little more than two hours' sleep. You need not speak of it; but Mrs. Fuller has not slept at all last night, and, through the effect of her hysterical complaints, she is,

at this time, as destitute of reason as an infant. My heart has not much sunk, because I look upon the derangement of her mind to be temporary; but the Lord knows what is before us![13]

Unfortunately, Fuller's hope that his wife's mental state would be temporary was not to be fulfilled. On July 25 Fuller cries out to God in the safe confines of his diary: "O my God, my soul is cast down within me! The afflictions in my family seem too heavy for me! O Lord, I am oppressed, undertake for me! My thoughts are broken off, and all my prospects seem to be perished!" During this time, Fuller drew encouragement from Scripture. He specifically cited biblical passages providing him support such as, "All things work together for good" (Rom. 8:28), "God, even our own God, shall bless us" (Ps. 67:6 KJV), and "It is of the LORD's mercies that we are not consumed" (Lam. 3:22 KJV).[14]

Throughout July and August of 1792, Sarah's mind was almost constantly confused. During these times, she considered her husband and her children as her worst enemies. Andrew Gunton Fuller, Fuller's son from his second marriage, records her deportment during this period.

She imagined that he was not her husband, but an imposter, who had entered the house and taken possession of all that belonged to her; supposing at other times that she had wandered from home, and had fallen among strangers. Her frequent attempts to escape rendered it necessary that she should be watched day and night.[15]

Two weeks before Sarah died, however, she had a period of clarity, much to the delight of her husband. Fuller describes their exchange in a letter to Sarah's father:

She had one of the happiest intervals of any during her affliction. She had been lamenting on account of this imposter that was come into her house, and would not give her the keys. She tried for two hours to obtain them by force, in which time she exhausted all her own strength and almost mine. Not being able to obtain her point, as I was necessarily obliged to resist her in this matter, she sat down and wept, threatening me that God would surely judge me for treating a poor helpless creature in such a manner! I also was overcome with grief; I wept with her. The sight of my tears seemed to awaken her recollection. With her eyes fixed upon me, she said: "Why, are you indeed my husband?" "Indeed, my dear, I am." "Oh, if I thought you were, I could give you a thousand kisses." "Indeed, my dear, I am your own dear husband." She then seated herself upon my knee and kissed me several times. My heart dissolved with mixture of grief and joy. Her senses were restored, and she talked as rationally as ever.[16]

On August 23, Fuller lost his wife of sixteen years. "Poor soul!" Fuller writes. "What she often said is now true. She was not at home . . . I am not her husband . . . these are not her children . . . but she has found her home . . . a home, a husband, and a family better than these."[17] Fuller had peace because he knew that Sarah was at peace. As difficult as this trial was, the most difficult still awaited Fuller.

Heartbreak of a Wayward Son

Andrew Gunton Fuller called the episode with Robert Fuller "a trial more severe even than that of losing his beloved wife."[18] Robert was Fuller's oldest son. He showed an early interest in the ministry. However, as Robert had not yet publicly professed faith in Christ, in May 1796 his father found him employment with a warehouse in London. He quickly lost that job, and Fuller helped him gain employment in Kettering. Once again, Robert failed to apply himself and demonstrated a tendency to restlessness. Robert's inability to hold down a job was a great cause of sorrow for his father, who writes to a friend:

> Those who have had no instruction, no pious example, no warnings or counsels, are often seen to be steady and trusty; but my child, who has had all these advantages, is worthy of no trust to be placed in him. I am afraid he will go into the army, that sink of immorality; or, if not, that being reduced to extremity, he will be tempted to steal. And, oh! if he should get such a habit, what may not these weeping eyes witness, or this broken heart be called to endure! O my God, whither will my fears lead me? Have mercy upon me, a poor unhappy parent! Have mercy upon him, a poor ungodly child![19]

Fuller's greatest fear was realized when Robert joined the army. Fuller was able to secure his discharge due to him being bound to an apprenticeship, but Robert immediately enlisted with the Marines. After serving two years, he wrote to his father expressing sorrow and seeking release. Again, Fuller secured his discharge. However, Robert's restless spirit was again unable to be satisfied, and his father secured a job for him aboard a merchant's ship. Before he could assume this new position, Robert was forced into service on a military ship. Not long after setting sail, Fuller received the horrifying report that Robert had been convicted of a misdemeanor, sentenced to three hundred lashes, and died from the severe punishment. When his father heard the news, he lamented in the words of David, "O Absalom! my son! my son! would I had died for thee, my son!" The report of Robert's death turned out to be false, but Fuller's trials with his son were far from over.[20]

Three years later, Robert deserted in Ireland and was punished so severely that he was unable to continue his tour on the sea. He eventually made his way home to his father, but before long he reenlisted in the Marines. Four years passed before Robert wrote to his father, who replied with an earnest appeal for his son's salvation. After assuring Robert of his forgiveness, Fuller pleads for his son's "repentance towards God and faith towards our Lord Jesus Christ, without which there is no forgiveness from above." He goes on to appeal to Robert's heart with the message of the mercy of Christ:

> You have had a large portion of God's preserving goodness, or you had ere now perished in your sins. Think of this, and give thanks to the father of mercies who has hitherto preserved you. Think, too, how you have requited Him, and be ashamed for all that you have done. Nevertheless, do not despair. Far as you have gone, and low as you are sunk in sin, yet if *from hence* you return to God by Jesus Christ, you will find mercy. Jesus Christ came into the world to save sinners, even the chief of sinners. If you had been ever so sober and steady in your behavior towards men, yet without repentance towards God and faith in Christ, you could not have been saved. And if you return to God by Him, though your sins be great and aggravated, you will find mercy.[21]

Subsequent letters from Robert gave the family some hope of his conversion, but there was still no certainty for them when they received word that Robert had perished off the coast of Lisbon, Spain, in March 1809. The day after the family received the news was the Lord's Day. Fuller preached from Romans 10:8–9 and took comfort from the following three thoughts:

> That the gospel is suited to *sinners of all degrees*, it asks not how long, or how often, or how greatly we have sinned; that it is suited to the *helpless condition of sinners*; that it is suited to sinners *in the last extremity*, it answers to the promised mercy in Deuteronomy 4:29: "*If from thence* thou shalt seek the Lord thy God, thou shalt find Him." Some are far from home, and have no friend in their dying moments to speak a word of comfort, but this is near. When Jonah was compassed about by the floods, when the billows and waves passed over him, he prayed the Lord, and the Lord heard him.[22]

At this point in the sermon, the anguished father apparently burst into tears.

In 1845, thirty years after the elder Fuller died, his son Andrew Gunton Fuller met a Mr. Waldy, a deacon of the Baptist church in Falkirk. Waldy told him that he knew his brother, Robert, while they were shipmates. Waldy and Robert had been close, and Waldy told Robert's younger brother that Robert had been "a very pleasing, nice youth, and became a true Christian man."[23] Perhaps in the end, Fuller's prayers for and pleading with Robert were answered by God. Although he never received this encouraging report, Fuller died believing that it was possible for his son to have been saved, even if he simply cried out to God for mercy in his final minutes.

School of Affliction

Fuller was a man who lived with great heartbreak throughout his ministry. In addition to his own physical maladies and weaknesses, he also endured the loss of a young child, the mental illness and eventual loss of a wife, and the agony of a wayward son. Fuller persevered through each of these trials with confidence in the sovereignty and goodness of God.

In his letter to Sarah's father informing him of her passing, Fuller signed it with the closing, "Yours, in great affliction."[24] Fuller endured this affliction, as all others, with confidence in God's sovereignty and goodness. He also clung to a view that the suffering of ministers was for their people's good. In a sermon preached eight years after Sarah's death from one of the texts that provided him comfort during his wife's illness (Rom. 8:28), Fuller expands on this idea:

> It is an interesting thought, that the afflictions of ministers are described in the Scriptures as generally sent them for the people's good. St. Paul speaks of the afflictions that befell him and his brethren as designed to qualify them to comfort others with the same comfort wherewith they themselves were comforted of God. . . . Perhaps the greatest qualifications, the best instruction, the most useful learning, that any Christian minister can attain, without any disparagement of other kinds of learning, is that which is attained in the school of affliction; it is by this he becomes able to feel, to sympathize, and to speak a word in season to them that are weary.[25]

The school of affliction is difficult, but it is God's ordained means of equipping his ministers for usefulness. Not only was Fuller faithful to God during his heartbreaking trials, but also God was being faithful to Fuller and his congregation by equipping him for greater usefulness through the means of trials and suffering. God still prepares his ministers in this way. May the example of Fuller encourage us to submit to this severe mercy as well as he did.

SEVEN

CHARLES SIMEON (1759–1836):
Faithful Shepherd to Hostile Sheep

RANDALL J. GRUENDYKE

They were all there. And why not? He had always been there for them. On the November afternoon of Charles Simeon's funeral, townsmen closed their shops and packed the main streets of Cambridge while hundreds of university gownsmen, for whom most lectures had been canceled that day, queued up three abreast in the King's College court. As the solemn line of mourners, led by dignitaries and family, slowly entered through the massive, west-facing doors of King's College Chapel, they were met by a tearful company from Holy Trinity Church, Simeon's congregation of fifty-four years. What followed was in keeping with Simeon's wishes—a simple service ending with "buri[al] in my college chapel," a place marked to this day by a cross pattée; his initials, CS; and the year 1836.

When one considers Simeon's accomplishments, it makes sense that the man for whom every Cambridge chapel bell tolled on that day was worthy of the honor. Even in human terms, Simeon was a thoroughgoing success. From his rooms in the Gibbs Building at King's, Simeon presided over his famous Friday evening "Conversation Parties"—a Q&A on the Bible and theology for generations of undergraduates. From that same place Simeon hosted his influential Sunday afternoon preaching classes—a clinic on sermon preparation and delivery that touched decades of aspiring ministers.

Through Holy Trinity Church, Simeon's strategic approaches to pastoral care, ministerial staffing, and Bible-centered preaching led to growth such that a meeting house was built at Market and Sidney Streets. As a leader in the church at large, Simeon advanced gospel proclamation by helping to found the Church Missionary Society. He also promoted the dissemination of Scripture by helping found the British and Foreign Bible Society and the popularity and influence of Bible exposition by publishing his sermons that, by the end of his life, totaled twenty-one volumes. Simeon also capitalized on an English ecclesiastical law that allowed him to appoint men of his choosing to pulpits throughout England.

But among those gathered on that soggy Saturday, there were some who remembered how it used to be—when Charles Simeon was among a despised and vast minority of evangelical Anglican ministers, when the name of the King's College fellow was a well-traveled term of derision (e.g., "Sim" or "Simeonite"), and when the perpetual curate of Holy Trinity Church was serving as a faithful shepherd among hostile sheep.

Privilege and Pain

Charles Simeon's early life was marked by seasons of privilege mixed with pain. He was born into privilege on September 24, 1759, but he suffered the pain of growing up without a mother. As a boy, Simeon was privileged to attend Eton, but as an adult he resolved that he would rather "murder" his own son than let him witness the evils he saw at the well-heeled prep school. As a King's Scholar at Eton, Simeon was privileged with admission to, as well as the exclusivities of, membership at King's College Cambridge. Simultaneously, the young scholar endured the pain of ostracism due to his evangelical faith, his conversion to which deserves some attention.

Other than a fleeting sense of pietistic devotion during a national fast day in 1776 for the beleaguered British troops fighting the "American War," young Simeon had little if any interest in spiritual things. That dramatically changed upon his entrance to King's when, in January 1779, Simeon learned that in three weeks he would be expected to attend the college communion service. The nineteen-year-old was mortified since, as he put it, "The thought rushed through my mind that Satan himself was as fit to attend as I."[1] In an attempt to soothe his disquieted soul, Simeon began voraciously reading religious literature.

He started with Richard Allestree's *The Whole Duty of Man* ("the only religious book that I had ever heard of,"[2] Simeon later recalled) and soon thereafter joined the Society for the Promotion of Christian Knowledge ("because I thought the books of that society would be the most useful of any I could procure"). While *Whole Duty* steadied Simeon to receive the February communion, it was a title by Bishop

Thomas Wilson, *A Short and Plain Instruction . . . of the Lord's Supper*, that God used to bring the nineteen-year-old to faith in Christ. Wilson helped Simeon see that just as the sins of God's Old Testament people were transferred to the head of a sacrificial animal, so the sins of his New Testament people, and Simeon in particular, had been entirely conveyed onto Christ. The brilliance of this good news rose like the sun in Simeon's heart so that "on the Wednesday [of Holy Week, I] began to have a hope of mercy; on the Thursday that hope increased; and on the Sunday morning, Easter Day, . . . I awoke early with those words upon my heart and lips, 'Jesus Christ is risen today! Hallelujah! Hallelujah!'"

While Simeon's newfound faith brought him great joy, it won him no friends. To be sure, there were other evangelicals in Cambridge at the time, but Simeon's gospel effusiveness (which earned him the disdainful descriptor *enthusiast*), coupled with the somewhat-cloistered life of a Kingsman (who enjoyed greater privileges than students at the other Cambridge colleges), kept him from meeting any of them. Though Simeon's predicament made for a lonely undergraduate life, it may have been those wilderness years that forced the new Christian to build and rely on his knowledge of Scripture as the source of his spiritual health.

Upon graduating from Cambridge, Simeon took up residence at King's College as a fellow and, four months later, was ordained as a deacon in the Church of England. That same year, Simeon began sitting under the ministry of Christopher Atkinson at nearby St. Edward King and Martyr. St. Edward's had been the furnace for the English Reformation, a fire stoked by Latimer, Barnes, and Bilney, among others. Now, 250 years later, most of that gospel heat was gone.

Nevertheless, when Atkinson invited Simeon to take his place for the summer of 1782, all that changed.

The brand-new Cambridge graduate filled the linenfold pulpit with Bible-centered sermons and a demonstrative preaching style that quickly upset the St. Edward's regulars. It also packed the remaining pews with more new faces than had been seen in a hundred years on Peas Hill. In a letter to pastor and hymn writer John Newton, John Berridge of Everton excitedly reported that since Simeon's arrival, St. Edward's was "crowded like a theater on the first night of a play."[3] Thus, it came as a significant surprise when Simeon's summer of privilege gave way to an extended season of pain.

Simeon's Trial

As an undergraduate, Simeon would walk through the center of Cambridge University, pass Holy Trinity Church, and wonder what it would be like to "preach the gospel there and be a herald for Him to the University."[4] In God's providence—and much to everyone's astonishment—that wish came true in the autumn of 1782. How that dream was realized led to what is arguably one of the most protracted trials ever suffered by a modern parish pastor.

Soon after learning about the sudden death of Holy Trinity's minister, Henry Therond, Simeon asked his father to put in a good word for him with the Bishop of Ely, James Yorke. Yorke was a friend of the elder Simeon's and was responsible for choosing Therond's successor. Richard Simeon expedited his son's request and, in short order, the bishop appointed the twenty-three-year-old Simeon to the Holy Trinity vacancy.

Upon hearing the name of their new pastor, the congregation erupted in protest and petitioned the bishop on behalf of their choice, John Hammond, who had at least three things weighing in his favor. First, Hammond was already ordained as a priest (Simeon was just a deacon) and had previously served a curacy at nearby St. Boltoph's. Second, Hammond had been a minister at Holy Trinity Church since Simeon was a schoolboy at Eton. Third, Hammond's broad theological views and political savvy were in keeping with the status quo of most Anglican churches of the time.

The bishop was so perturbed by the people's plea, which he supposed to be a challenge to his authority, that he wrote to the young Simeon and said the job was his, and that even if Simeon had resigned (as falsely reported by the congregation to the bishop), Hammond would not be selected to serve as the next minister of Holy Trinity. Yorke's letter sealed both Simeon's appointment and the people's opposition to him. In defiance of the bishop's decision, and per their prerogative, the congregation hired Hammond as their afternoon lecturer and gave him a salary twice that of Simeon. The battle line had been drawn, and neither the people nor their leader, Hammond, was prepared to budge.

Even though Simeon's new charge was just a three-minute walk from the scene of his summer success, it must have seemed like a million miles when he first stepped into the Holy Trinity Church pulpit on November 10. The resentful congregation welcomed Simeon by locking their rented pews and refusing to show up. Anyone coming to hear the new preacher had to sit in the aisles in which Simeon had set up seats at his own expense. In response to this accommodation, the church wardens tossed the seats out of the building and into the street. This led Simeon to start a Sunday evening service. At first, the church wardens opposed it, so Simeon backed off. The next year he tried to launch it again and was presented with a statement from church officers declaring that Holy Trinity had never held a third service and was in no way predisposed to do so. When Simeon tried a third time, the church wardens retaliated by locking the church doors.

Opponents at the University

Simeon was opposed not only by the people of his own parish but also by the members of his own university. When the church wardens finally agreed to let Simeon start a Sunday night service, the university scheduled a Greek lecture at the same hour. The establishment hoped to discourage students from sitting under Simeon's gospel-centered preaching. For the undergraduates who did make it to hear Simeon, there was a price to be paid. To avoid harm from hecklers, gownsmen traveled to and from Holy Trinity Church in groups.

Following each service, Simeon or the church moderator, William Farish, stood by the north door to prevent altercations between loitering troublemakers and departing churchgoers. Despite their best efforts, stones were thrown outside the building while periodic distractions, including a drunken disturbance, took place inside. On at least one occasion, Simeon was pelted with rotten eggs. On another, he escaped being jumped at the north door when he uncustomarily departed through the south exit. Years later, recalling Simeon's early days at Holy Trinity Church, William Dealtry said, "Within these sacred walls disorders have occurred which it required the greatest vigor, and most determined resolution to put down."[5]

For a dozen years Simeon faithfully shepherded his persistently hostile flock. So recalcitrant was the membership that it circulated one petition after another demanding their minister's removal. Pastoral visitation was futile. And when, after five years, Hammond finally resigned his afternoon lectureship, the congregation bypassed Simeon and hired Butler Berry to replace Hammond. Berry held the post for seven years. In 1795 the entrenched opposition finally ended, and while never entirely free from trials (e.g., a compromised state of health hampered him in middle age from 1807 to 1820), Simeon's best days were ahead of him. But he had suffered for twelve long years.

Simeon's Response

To be sure, most ministers would wilt under such hostility. What steadied Simeon during that epic time of testing? At least three things, all of them lessons for today's pastor who either is or will be under the lash of persecution—perhaps even at the hands of his own congregation.

Simeon Held On to the Word and Prayer

Simeon clung tightly to the essential means of grace—the Word and prayer—and his everyday schedule reflected that priority. While not an early riser by nature, Simeon became one by choice for the purpose of prayerfully saturating himself in Scripture. A former roommate and witness of Simeon's daily routine once attested that he regularly rose at 4:00 a.m. Years later, Matthew Preston, one of Simeon's curates, observed the same, noting, "He rose very early—for that purpose retiring early to rest."[6] Devoting the first four hours of his day to the Lord (the privilege of a lifelong bachelor),

Simeon was able to prayerfully consider his life circumstances in light of God's Word. Concerning the hostile congregation of Holy Trinity Church, he reflects:

> In this state of things, I saw no remedy but faith and patience. The passage of Scripture which subdued and controlled my mind was this, "The servant of the Lord must not strive" (2 Tim. 2:24). It was painful indeed to see the church, with the exception of the aisles, almost forsaken; but I thought that if God would only give a double blessing to the congregation that did attend, there would . . . be as much good done as if the congregation were doubled and the blessing limited to only half the amount. Without such a reflection, I should have sunk under the burden.[7]

From his sermons, it is clear that one of Simeon's favorite verses was Psalm 81:10: "I am the LORD thy God, which brought thee out of the land of Egypt: open thy mouth wide, and I will fill it" (KJV). In the midst of his hardship, Simeon recommended that believers walk close with God, read his Word much, and pray much.

Simeon Held On to Humility

Upon Simeon's appointment to Holy Trinity, business magnate and evangelical statesman John Thornton advised the young minister that "to soar heavenward" he must "grow downwards in humility."[8] Simeon took Thornton's words, along with those of other eminent well-wishers, to heart and submitted himself to the same church wardens who hated him. Simeon reasoned, "I wished rather to suffer than to act; because in suffering I could not fail to be right; but in acting I might easily do amiss."[9]

Simeon's reactive posture of humility was shaped by his proactive practice of the same. Throughout his early years, the young pastor humbly sought the counsel of elder clergymen, especially Henry Venn, in matters of life and ministry. Simeon also put his preaching under the scrutiny of a Mr. Rilands, whom he describes as "a faithful friend," since only such a friend would "show you your deficiencies."[10] Later, Venn writes to Rilands, "None can bear and receive profit from reproof like [Charles Simeon]."[11] During this painful period, Simeon carried in his wallet the humble reminder "Talk not about myself," and in 1788 he observes, "The three lessons that a minister has to learn, 1. Humility—2. Humility—3. Humility."[12]

At a point in life when Simeon was "more conspicuous for his courage and energy than his discretion," the Lord honored the young minister's commitment to humility by preventing his passion from ever harming his work.[13]

Simeon Held On to His Ministry

The hostility of Simeon's church did not tempt him to walk away from his ministry. If those who rented the pews at Holy Trinity Church stubbornly refused to fill them on Sunday morning, then Simeon gratefully preached to the men and women who gladly filled the aisles. Most of them were university students, the working class, and residents of the parish house who, if they hoped to eat, were required by law to attend church twice on Sunday. Simeon also began to preach in modest village congregations. He even delivered early morning sermons to farmhands who gathered in a nearby barn. Around this same time, Simeon used Sunday afternoons to teach future ministers how to preach.

Simeon held on to and advanced his ministry outside of the pulpit as well. When the church wardens at Holy Trinity prevented parishioners from meeting with Simeon in their building, the young minister rented a room in town. And during this time Simeon successfully started a youth group as well as a network of affinity-based small groups, the leaders of which Simeon supervised on a monthly basis. Even during those difficult years, Simeon regularly donated a third of his income to advance the ministries of others, including those dedicated to church schools, local pastors, needy widows, and more. Simeon refused to let the opposition inhibit his ministry to all. And he certainly kept what was happening within the flock from preventing what could be done outside.

Simeon's Legacy

In Charles Simeon's early days of ministry, it appeared that the people of Holy Trinity Church opposed him because they wanted John Hammond to be their minister. That was partly true, but over time it became apparent that their hostility was largely "due to the directness of [Simeon's] Gospel preaching."[14]

Gratefully, Simeon's suffering did not frustrate the Lord's work in and through him as, over time, he was rewarded for his pastoral faithfulness and tenacity. Simeon's devotion to the good news strengthened the Trinity pulpit as well as her people. His ministerial example was followed by numerous protégés who furthered gospel proclamation throughout Great Britain and beyond. Simeon's ministry set a standard for ministers and gospel workers not only in his lifetime but beyond it as well.

Today, the ministries of Universities and Colleges Christian Fellowship (UCCF) in the United Kingdom, InterVarsity Christian Fellowship (IVCF) in the United States, and International Fellowship of Evangelical Students (IFES) elsewhere in the world can trace the roots of their university-based ministries back to the enduring influence of Charles Simeon. And around the globe, the broadly influential ministries of Phillip Jensen (Australia), Dick Lucas and the late John Stott (England), and Kent Hughes (United States) have Simeon's gospel fingerprints all over them—ongoing testimonies to a faithful shepherd among hostile sheep and to the Great Shepherd by whom he was steadied and sustained.

EIGHT

JOHN CHAVIS (1763-1838): Faithful in the Face of Racism

DARRYL WILLIAMSON

O n a warm Sunday afternoon in August 1831, seven Negro slave men met for an afternoon barbecue in the woods on the plantation of Joseph Travis in Southampton County, Virginia. Their conversation lasted nearly eleven hours and was led by a strong and religious-minded slave named Nat Turner. Turner believed God had signaled him to lead an insurrection to overturn the evil of slavery. Later that evening, Turner and a band of sixty slaves attempted to make that vision a reality.

Over the course of forty-eight hours, this violent troop went from house to house, killing fifty-five white men, women, and children. After shootouts with groups of white men and some of their black slaves, many of the rebels were killed, and Turner himself was captured and subsequently hanged on November 11. He was then beheaded and publicly mutilated as a warning to other would-be rebels.

Nat Turner's rebellion produced fear in white Americans all over the South, causing many to see every black person, slave or free, as a violent threat. Both Virginia and North Carolina passed laws making it a crime to teach blacks—literacy was thought to be a significant factor in rebellious thinking. North Carolina went further, preventing all blacks, whether slave or free, from preaching, teaching, or leading any gathering.

These new laws institutionalized white fear. Legal freedom did not protect black citizens from being lumped in with slaves, since they all shared the one thing that mattered most in the minds of white Southerners—they were Negro. Free blacks who lived productive and noble lives alongside their white neighbors were vulnerable in the face of the fearful impulses of racism. Even a black man of well-known spiritual character and who counted among his closest friends and acquaintances leading white citizens could find himself defenseless to racialized fears and irrational overreaction.

That was the experience of early nineteenth-century African American Presbyterian preacher and well-respected educator John Chavis.

Breaking Stereotypes

John Chavis does not fit the modern-day stereotype of a black man in eighteenth-century North Carolina. Though the precise details of his birth and early life are often debated, Chavis was born in either 1762 or 1763 and descended from free black settlers of Granville County, Virginia. His ancestors were property owners and were educated and respected in their communities, volunteering to serve in defense of American freedom as militiamen throughout the colonial period. Chavis himself would later serve three years in the American Revolutionary War.

Chavis likely was reared near the Presbyterian settlement of free blacks in North Carolina known as White Hall. Tom Blackwell, the principal landowner in the settlement, advocated for education, so there were cultural influences that would have helped Chavis value education. Additionally, Chavis's ancestors were literate, so education was evidently a valued part of his family's legacy.

There is some indication that John Chavis may have spent a fair part of his childhood as an indentured servant in the home of the Rev. William Willie, apparently a renaissance man with an abundant supply of books covering a wide array of topics. If Chavis spent several childhood years in Willie's home, he would have had ample opportunity to stimulate his intellectual curiosity from that vast library and to interact with Willie himself. That a young black boy would have been raised in the North Carolina home of an esteemed white family in the 1770s says much about the respect Chavis's family had in the community. And like for many white immigrants, indentured servitude would be a path Chavis would take to ensure himself a solid footing in his pursuit of all that American liberty had to offer.

There is great reason to believe that Chavis spent his later childhood and early teen years under the tutelage of the esteemed Presbyterian minister Henry Patillo as a student in the Latin grammar school he ran called Granville Hall. Patillo was a patriot and an influential pastor. Many of his students were moved by his enthusiasm for the American Republic and enlisted in the Revolutionary War cause.

In a spirit of patriotism, Chavis enlisted in the Continental Army in 1780 at the age of seventeen, which was unusual for a young black man as they were not typically seen as friendly toward the patriot cause in colonial times. No doubt, Chavis's family legacy as property owners factored into his enlistment success. Chavis thus served faithfully in the revolutionary cause for three years.

His identity and credentials as an American patriot and valuable citizen can hardly be denied. This is seen not only by his service to the new nation but also by his membership in the elite quarters of colonial and early American society. He was clearly seen, treated, and respected by whites as a social and cultural equal.

Keen Mind, Gifted Preacher

After the war, Chavis went on to serve as a Latin and Greek tutor and continually impressed everyone he encountered with his academic promise and potential. He was eventually sent to study at Princeton as the private student of its president, John Witherspoon. Witherspoon had signed the Declaration of Independence and greatly valued open and free inquiry. Chavis was nurtured in a Presbyterian faith anchored in intellectual rigor and a robust commitment to the American republic. And though he did not graduate from Princeton—completing his academic studies at Washington College in Virginia—he benefited from the young nation's best ministerial minds, and he won their confidence in his ability and character.

As hard as it is to believe from our twenty-first-century vantage point, the overwhelming majority of blacks in post-colonial America were unconverted and superstitious. This was especially true on large Southern plantations at which the slave populations dwarfed the numbers of whites. Though for many years there had been resistance to evangelizing African slaves, by the end of the eighteenth century many Presbyterian ministers were under conviction to proclaim the gospel to them, and Chavis's mentor, Patillo, was of that mind.

Patillo advocated for Chavis. He recognized in Chavis the graces of gospel ministry and occasionally opened his pulpit to Chavis to preach. In 1799, with Patillo's support as well as the support of others, Chavis applied for ministerial appointment to the Lexington presbytery and was examined. In October 1800 Chavis became the first black man in America licensed to preach by the Presbyterian Church.

Understandably, Chavis was charged with preaching to the black masses in the South to remedy the spiritual darkness among them, believing he could do a better job in reaching them than white ministers could. However, Chavis's labors were more often expended with white audiences as he traveled back and forth on horseback to various congregations. It has been said that Chavis's speech was free of Negroisms.[1] The enthusiastic reception he received from white congregations suggests his voice was heard with spiritual authority and that the faith of many was encouraged by his preaching and teaching.

Not long after Chavis's commissioning as an itinerant preacher in the Presbyterian Church he completed his formal studies. Leveraging his success as an effective Latin and

Greek tutor and his sterling reputation as a minister, Chavis opened a classical school in 1805 in Raleigh, North Carolina.

Continuing to challenge our modern-day assumptions, he taught white and black children together in an integrated setting. By 1808, like the gathering of cultural storm clouds, the parents of Chavis's white students began to complain and insist that their children not be taught with black children. Chavis accommodated this demand by creating a day school for white children and an evening school for black children, with the latter having slightly lower tuition.

Still, Chavis enjoyed a buoyant reputation. His white students were among North Carolina's aristocracy, and many of those who came up under his instruction became statesmen, influential businessmen, and scholars in their own rights. Most of Chavis's students retained the highest admiration for him. Willie P. Mangum would become a US senator and eventually its legislative leader. He was a close friend of Chavis until his death. Charles Manley would later be governor of North Carolina. Abraham Mencher went on to serve as minister (ambassador) to Portugal and eventually territorial governor of New Mexico.

Man of Society

It would be a mistake to see the career attainments of his former students as signs merely of Chavis's teaching prowess, which he undeniably possessed. Instead, these luminaries also indicate the heights Chavis had personally attained as a black man in North Carolina society. Between 1805 and 1830, the state's wealthiest and most influential white families entrusted the education and character formation of their children to this black man. They knew him well and revered him.

There is good reason today to believe that Chavis is buried on the family property of Senator Mangum's parents. Correspondence between Chavis and men such as Mangum reflects familiar cordiality and intellectual equality, with Chavis's tone still reflecting the posture of tutor.

Controversial Legacy

It is easy to understand why the legacy of Chavis was a controversial topic at the end of the nineteenth century after the Civil War and following Reconstruction as black codes and Jim Crow laws were established against the new freedmen. These discriminations were defended among gentlemen because of the assumed inferiority of the Negro. However, if black people possessed the same capabilities and virtues as white men and women, denying them basic freedoms would be patently indefensible.

Providence soon acquainted Chavis with the reality that in America's racialized society, even close friends of different racial backgrounds saw the world through different emotional lenses. What prompted fear in white Americans often produced anger among blacks. Fears and concerns that leapt in the hearts of American Negroes were often the flipside to the same circumstances that brought relief and celebration to white hearts. This was the emotional landscape in the South before and after the Nat Turner rebellion.

In 1800, Gabriel Prosser had planned a slave rebellion in Richmond, Virginia, which was foiled when a slave told his master of the plans, leading to Prosser's eventual capture and hanging. The year 1822 saw the arrest and execution of Denmark Vessey in Charleston, South Carolina, as his plot to lead a slave insurrection was also uncovered and thwarted. In 1829, an out-of-state white minister circulated a letter in North Carolina that many took to be a call for slave rebellion. The letter was David Walker's famous "Appeal to the Colored Citizens of the World," which underscored the inhumanity of slavery and called black people to claim their rightful place in the world of civilized men by decisive action, moral improvement, and hard work.[2]

White people feared that Walker's letter would lead to violence. When Chavis, who had become a spokesman for black people, was asked by several slaveholders of Orange County about the letter and its preaching of open rebellion, Chavis boldly replies, "I am not surprised. It is very possible that violence could erupt under the present dangerous circumstances."[3]

Following Nat Turner's rebellion, Chavis wrote to his former student Willie Mangum, who was serving at the time as a congressman, saying he didn't believe Turner guilty of the charges against him and that his hanging was a travesty of justice. Chavis's position was anchored in his belief that the criminal justice system was inherently unfair to black people. And his letter was no doubt intended to use the social and relationship capital he believed he had with Congressman Mangum to pursue the just cause of defending American blacks from unfair treatment.

Perhaps a more strategically thoughtful response to the slaveholders regarding Walker's letter would have included assurances that slave insurrection was unlikely, at least in North Carolina. Maybe if Chavis had exhorted those men to meet their concerns, not with threats and restrictions but with kind considerations and cordiality toward their slaves, a less hostile mindset might have ruled the day. Whatever might have been, Turner's swift and violent revolt provided all the clarity these men needed.

In 1832 the North Carolina legislature enacted a law for the "better regulation of the conduct of Negroes, slaves and free persons of color." A 1930 scholarly journal noted that

> the statute made it unlawful for any free Negro, slave or free person of color to preach or exhort in public or in any matter to officiate as preacher or teacher . . . where slaves of different families were collected together. Any free Negro or free person of color who was duly convicted or indicted . . . [is] for each offence to receive not exceeding thirty-nine lashes on his bare back.[4]

In a stroke of administrative muscle, the legal ground on which Chavis operated and provided for his family had quaked beneath him. All the securities that education, character, hard work, and reputation promised were erased in a flash by a law that seemed written with him in mind. No one had called John Chavis a derogatory name. He had not been threatened with violence. None of the actions commonly designated as racist were directly employed against him. Yet if God endowed all men with the unalienable rights of life, liberty, and the pursuit of happiness, Chavis was exempted even in the face of his literal defense of that principle. Because he was forbidden from teaching black students and from preaching to black congregants, Chavis's white-student families quickly removed their children from his tutelage, and his employments were a memory.

Great Voice Silenced

Given the seriousness of his new situation—unable to preach or teach—Chavis appealed to the Orange County presbytery for their intervention. But they were in full submission to and no doubt in agreement with the new law. The official response from the presbytery to Chavis in his predicament reads as follows: "Resolved, that the Presbytery in view of all the circumstances of the case recommend to [John Chavis] to acquiesce in the decision of the Legislature referred until God in his providence shall open to him the path of duty, in regard to exercise of his ministry."[5]

There are many ironies in this response, chief among them that many of the leaders in the presbytery would have no doubt either fought in the Revolutionary War or at least revered those who did. As such they were quick to act in the interest of their freedom. Another irony is the similar lack of patience in the wise providence of God they would all soon display in the decisions leading to secession and the Civil War. It is hard to deny their counsel was less grounded in theology and more rooted in a lack of empathy for Chavis's situation. And rooted in the belief that the appropriate response to one black man's malevolent act is to limit the actions of all black men.

When he was unable to teach or preach and therefore unable to sustain a livelihood for his family, he appealed to the Orange County presbytery for help. That request was met with a collection providing him $52.42, while also unspeakably suspending his license to preach. For a man of Chavis's stature and achievement, becoming a ward of the presbytery would be a great blow to his dignity, when his only infirmity was his skin color.

Response

Chavis's response to his situation was to confront it with grit and determination. He first tried to resume teaching by offering to tutor the children of his former student Willie Mangum, then serving in Congress and later the Senate. Chavis sent many letters over a few years to Mangum, most of which were unanswered. Though Chavis tried to maintain a gentlemanly tone, his frustration seeps through: "Is it my color, or my insignificance or the gross ignorance, which my many letters contain, the reason you have not condescended to answer one of them? Or is it your distrust of my professed, firm, unshaken, unabating friendship for you and your family? Or do you consider my friendship to be not worthy your notice?"[6]

What is most striking in this September 1831 letter from Chavis to Mangum was Chavis's segue from personal offense to political commentary. He exhorts Mangum to resist political friendship with "[Andrew] Jackson" and to "put on again your full coat of Federalism" and "support the renewal of the United States bank."[7] As a modern reader, it is difficult to discern whether this is general concern in the political fortunes of a former charge or a form of self-denial of his lower and dependent status. Perhaps it is simply Chavis's desperate attempt to remind Mangum and himself that he is still a distinguished American.

In March 1832, still having not heard back from Senator Mangum, Chavis wrote again. In closing the letter, he mentions other former students: "Please give my respects to my son Abraham Rencher and to General Barringer, and tell them I would be glad to receive a letter from them. Tell them if I am Black I am free born American and a revolutionary soldier and therefore ought not to be thrown entirely out of the scale of notice."[8] These sentiments would, of course, be echoed throughout American history as black soldiers served valiantly in World Wars I and II and yet returned home to disrespect and racial violence.

Failure of Brotherly Love

Was Chavis a victim of racism? No doubt. Lumping free and slave blacks into a single class regardless of their education, actions, or Christian pedigree made blackness itself a moral category, justifying corrective action targeting blackness. This brings to mind the observations of esteemed historian Mark Noll that the slavery question for Christians in the United States was never about the right interpretation of Scripture but always a question of the full deposit of humanity in black men and women.[9]

The racism Chavis experienced was ultimately a breakdown in brotherly love. That's what makes racism and betrayal both sinful and discouraging—it violates the biblical admonition of love to neighbor, which in turn violates the biblical admonition of love to God. Those closest to Chavis betrayed him, and it was hurtful and perplexing. It's always difficult to comprehend permanent fractures between brothers when Scripture brims with admonitions to forgive one another and warnings as to what will happen if these relationships remain unreconciled (Eph. 4:32; Matt. 18:15–35). Still, Chavis soldiered on in ministry in spite of relational dynamics and injustices that were difficult to swallow.

Chavis died in 1838, and the circumstances of his death are clouded in speculation. There is no triumphant moment in his story, no sense that he or his friends overcame the racism of his times. Racism, it seems, won the day. One thinks of the apostle Paul spending his remaining days in the Mamertine Prison in Rome, cold and alone, reflecting on his being abandoned, not by his enemies, but by his friends.

Shouting out to us from the early nineteenth century, John Chavis's story summons us as Christians to examine our actions in the face of injustice, especially its systemic manifestations. When we consider Christian biography, we are often caught up in the heroism of individuals and often neglect the spiritual cowardice of the church and culture. Chavis's account prompts us to cast our gaze more broadly so that we might see in our time not only the exceptionalism of an individual but also the character and weaknesses of the church.

NINE

C. H. SPURGEON (1834-92):
Faithful in Sorrow

ZACK ESWINE

On Sunday evenings, after he'd completed his work from the week and the day, Charles Spurgeon and his wife, Susannah, would find some quiet and sit together. Spurgeon served as pastor of Victorian London's largest congregation, New Park Street Baptist Church. Inevitably, Susannah would ask, "Dear, should I read to you tonight?" If Charles felt particularly glad for the work of the day, if he felt that he had been faithful to the God he loved, he would say, "Yes, Wifey [that was one of his affectionate names for Susannah]. That would be very refreshing. Would you mind reading a page or two of good George Herbert?" As Susannah read, her husband's mental and physical fatigue would subside. Sleep would come easy that night.[1]

It isn't that Spurgeon was unaccustomed to the hard work of ministry. He had been preaching since he was a teenager.

Wherever Spurgeon preached, larger sanctuaries became necessary, and were ultimately built, to accommodate the swelling numbers of people who came to hear him. He was a phenom of the time. This meant that critics made their disappointment publicly and regularly known. On many Sunday nights, the fatigue that battled Spurgeon was more than physical. According to Susannah, her husband could be "sorely depressed in spirit following the ministry of the day."[2] He felt as though his faithfulness fell short of God's worthy and lovely character. Out of his anguish of heart, he'd ask his wife to read the sober exhortations of Richard Baxter's *The Reformed Pastor*. She would read page after page of Baxter's concern for an unconverted clergy and his stern pleadings regarding the sobering and high calling of a minister's work in Christ. According to Susannah, her husband would burst into "heart sobs," weeping deep in his soul over the "smitings of a very tender conscience toward God." She would cry with him, out of tender love for him. She felt that he was harder on himself than was warranted, so often having no legitimate cause for the way he upbraided his soul.

Spiritual Sorrows

Charles Spurgeon used the term *fainting fits*[3] to describe our experiences with sorrow. Sorrows sometimes have a spiritual source. Spiritually, we depress. We feel as though we've displeased God and have no remedy, as when Spurgeon was weighed down by guilt over a sermon on a Sunday night. At other times, spiritual depression haunts us for years as it did the poet William Cowper, whom Spurgeon esteemed. The same man who wrote, "Behind a frowning providence,

[God] hides a smiling face,"[4] would also describe himself as worse than a castaway without God and dying at sea in shipwreck.

> No voice divine the storm allayed,
> No light propitious shone;
> When, snatched from all effectual aid,
> We perished, each alone;
> But I beneath a rougher sea,
> And whelmed in deeper gulfs than he.[5]

These "spiritual sorrows," Spurgeon says, "are the worst of mental miseries."[6] We either believe God has deserted us and left us barren in his absence, or we think God is gleefully present, happily smiting us with our actual guilt and delighting as we squirm in agony with no mercy and no way out.[7] These are the worst kind of sorrows. Spurgeon felt that a person can learn to bear with a bleeding body or in time get through their wounds of soul, but spiritual sorrows prove nearly too much to endure.[8]

At such times, Spurgeon reminds us that preaching the bountiful aid of the cross or the empty tomb or Jesus's ascension will provide no felt relief or respite. Only the Garden of Gethsemane can free us in our anguish.[9] For there, we do not have a general who stands in the back in safety demanding that we weary ones charge first into battle. On the contrary, the garden of betrayal shows us our fellow friend who steps forward to take the lead. He runs toward the fight before all of us. He faces the enemy first so that we who follow are neither alone nor without hope. We see him sweat blood drops. We watch the cheek-kisser betray his love for coins. Torchlight rouses the courage of the cowardly. They bind our Lord and mock him till dawn. So we preach this Christ of the garden, and the spiritually haunted discover the God who walks their path of mental misery, who feels their pains of anguished burden, and who beckons their comradery as fellow sufferers who overcome.

Circumstantial Sorrows

Spurgeon's honesty about his sufferings and his open compassion for the sufferings of others can catch us off guard. After all, he was one of history's first megachurch pastors. He preached as a Reformed Baptist to thousands each week during the nineteenth-century Victorian era in England. His messages were printed weekly in local periodicals, which meant thousands upon thousands accessed his sermons. He started various ministries and new churches, including a pastors' college and orphanages. He offered then and now a model of ministerial success to many. Yet Spurgeon was a man transparently acquainted with terrible sorrows in body and soul. He was an imperfect man who looked to the same Savior he preached to us.

The sorrows Spurgeon experienced were not only spiritual in nature. He also named circumstances as a terrible source of sadness.

One wounding incident spooked Spurgeon all his life. On October 19, 1856, as he stood in the pulpit preaching to thousands, a prankster yelled, "Fire!" The resulting panic left seven dead and twenty-eight seriously injured. Spurgeon was only twenty-two years old at the time. He and Susannah had married ten months before and were diaper-deep into the first month of parenting their twin boys in a new house full of unpacked boxes. With so many people dead, newspapers across London cruelly and mercilessly blamed him. No one knew if Spurgeon would preach again—he considered quitting. Susannah says that her husband tottered on the verge of insanity. Those close to him provided what we would call today a suicide watch to make sure he didn't harm himself in his despair.

Twenty-five years later, Spurgeon was about to address a large audience during a session of the Baptist Union. He was older now, middle-aged, a seasoned pastor and widely known. With all seats accounted for, hundreds pressed in. Spurgeon walked onto the platform and became "entirely un-manned . . . leaning his head on his hand."[10] He experienced what we call a flashback or a post-trauma response. The present moment triggered a haunting memory. Spurgeon's body responded as if threatened by danger. He preached that night but barely. Frowning providences sometimes don't take the hint and move on. They lurk and loiter around our memory for years.

Spurgeon suggests that broken hearts come in several ways:

- desertion—neglect or betrayal by a spouse, family member, or friend
- bereavement—ailment or death of one we love
- penury—job loss, financial strain, poverty of basic needs
- disappointment and defeat—dreams unreached, goals blocked, attempts that failed, foes who won
- guilt—regrets, pains we've caused others, sins against God

Further, Spurgeon said, we are like the victim of a crime. Say, for example, an intruder entered our homes and ransacked the living room and took all we held dear away from us while some of our neighbors slept and others sought entertainment among the late-night reruns. The circumstances leave a mark, the kind of scar that takes nearly a lifetime to fade. But grace doesn't quit.

For a time after the prank, if Spurgeon saw a Bible it made him cry. Yet he did preach again and care for Susannah and the twins again, one day at a time with Jesus. Listen in. Hear this small, adult-sized step of grace as he preached again for the first time after the circumstance that mobbed him like a gang to loot his sanity:

> I almost regret this morning that I have ventured to occupy this pulpit because I feel utterly unable to preach to you for your profit. I had thought that the quiet and repose of the last fortnight had removed the effects of that terrible catastrophe; but on coming back to the same spot again, and more especially, standing here to address you, I feel somewhat of those same painful emotions which well-nigh prostrated me before. You will, therefore, excuse me this morning. . . . I have been utterly unable to study. . . . Oh, Spirit of God, magnify thy strength in thy servant's weakness and enable him to honor his Lord, even when his soul is cast down within him.[11]

How do we overcome? One imperfect, frazzled, vulnerable step at a time. We get honest about the effects of circumstances. We endure remnants of painful emotion and bodily anxiety. We cry out from our souls to God and take hold of what has always been true but what we didn't live out before. Our greatest hope at this moment isn't the absence of our weakness but the presence of God's strength.

Biological Sorrows

Spurgeon applied what a Christian theology of persons taught him. A person is a "double being," he would say. We are body and soul.[12] We experience injuries and hurts that arise from spiritual and circumstantial sources. But our bodies can also promote sorrows. If spiritual pains seize upon our conscience and mental sorrows rise from negative circumstances, biological sorrows originate in our bodily chemistry. "Some persons are constitutionally sad," Spurgeon says. "They are marked with melancholy from their birth."[13]

A Christian theology of the body in a fallen world reminds us that sorrow is not itself a sin. Sorrow is a sane response to what is fallen. Spurgeon also says that depression is more of a misfortune than a fault. For these reasons, there are times when prayers, promises, Scripture reading, counsel, and preaching are not enough to help us. Not because these gifts from God are without power in Jesus to relieve and heal us, but because the medicine prescribed doesn't fit the source of the problem. Soul remedies for bodily ailments are necessary but incomplete. What does this mean? Those of us with bodily origins for our depression can follow Spurgeon's lead as he sought remedy and help:

- We need to adjust our work rhythms and expectations. Spurgeon resisted this change at first, but gradually began to take regular breaks for months at a time in Mentone, France. For the sake of his health and ministry, such breaks were wise. He also used regular hot baths to relax his body and mind.
- We need to build into our lives regular rhythms with God's creation. Communion with nature eased the gloom

and fatigue that the fog, frost, and damp of London agitated amid the pain of work. The cold, wet days of winter acted upon his sensitive frame. Dull and dreary days depressed him. His urban ministry required rural retreats to keep him flourishing.

- We need laughter. Our trouble isn't like the trouble of those who cannot cry and resist the sanity of sadness. Our trouble is that we cannot rest from seeing beauty in all beauty's feisty, God-given refusal to quit when things go dark. On the advice of Proverbs 17:22, Spurgeon intentionally sought out stories of good humor and gracious strength. He read them, collected them, and told them.

- We need to pay attention to how food and drink affect our melancholy. Spurgeon spoke of how he had to learn about the effects of what he ate.

- We need to use medicine, not as a cure or as our "go to" but as one teammate with these others, to help us wisely navigate the sorrows our bodies prompt until Jesus comes again.[14] Medicine is like the sixth person on a starting team of five. When a starter needs a breather, the sixth person comes off the bench to support and maintain the team for significant minutes.

Bringing Harm in the Name of Help

Incompleteness and impatience among Christians often inflict a double wound to those who suffer sorrows. Our biblical framework reveals its incompleteness when we do not account for spiritual, circumstantial, or biological contributors to the sorrows of those we try to help. Our impatience shows itself in our trite answers and quick remedies. We become like Job's friends, incomplete in our understanding and impatient with healing. We say true things in all the wrong ways and at all the wrong times. Spurgeon often spoke, openly and forcefully, against those harmful helpers who say to the depressed: "Oh! You should not feel like this!" or "Oh! You should not speak such words, nor think such thoughts."[15]

"Ah!" says one, "I used to laugh at Mrs. So-and-so for being nervous; now that I feel the torture myself, I am sorry that I was ever hard on her." "Ah!" says another, "I used to think of such-and-such a person that he must be a fool to be always in so gloomy a state of mind; but now I cannot help sinking into the same desponding frames, and oh! I would to God that I had been more kind to him!" Yes, we should feel more for the prisoner if we knew more about the prison.[16]

A raised voice and trite sayings cannot mend another human being. We look to Jesus with our consciences, our circumstances, and our chemistries. The sorrowing have a Savior. Our sturdy hope isn't that we get ourselves together but that he holds us and all things together, whether we find assurance or not. Our healing isn't what saves us. His grace saves us. Our speedy recovery isn't what gives us hope. His unselfish willingness to find us and carry us home anchors the hope on which we lean.

Even those who contemplate taking their lives hear Spurgeon's appeal for life only after Spurgeon shares with them his desire to die and his surprise that in this fallen world more of us haven't ended it all. In this fellow-feeling of a friend, who himself is acquainted with the abysmal darkness,

Spurgeon then lifts his and our hope to the Man of sorrows sent from God—God himself. The Man of sorrows not only pays for our sins but also takes our howling cry up to God, "Why have you forsaken me?" The sorrowing have a savior because the Savior is also acquainted with grief, wondering why God would let the pain go unanswered.

The God we turn to has turned first to us. He comes as a humbled one who also has suffered. We look to him for help, for healing, and for hope. The sorrowing Savior fought death to the death and won.

Run to the Fight

Where does this leave us? Spurgeon as a fellow sorrower calls out to us:

> The soul is broken in pieces, lanced, pricked with knives, dissolved, racked, pained. It knows not how to exist when it gives way to fear. Up, Christian! You are of a sorrowful countenance; up and chase your fears. Why would you be ever groaning in your dungeon? Why should Giant Despair forever beat you with his Crabtree cudgel? Up! Drive him away![17]

But how? If our greatest hope isn't our present healing but his everlasting love, what do we do? With all of his promises, words, counsel, and saving graces; with all of his natural provisions of retreat, laughter, creation, quiet, rest, hot baths, and medicines; with every cavernous longing for the redemption of every aching thing—we look at our accuser, and we whisper if we cannot shout: "You might be right, but Jesus!"

You might be right, things are worse than I thought,
   but Jesus!

You might be right, all is lost, but Jesus!

You might be right, I am abandoned, but Jesus!

You might be right, I am forfeit, but Jesus!

You might be right, I should stay down, but Jesus!

You might be right, it would be too late for me, but Jesus!

You might be right, I am out of reach, but Jesus!

You might be right, I am a sinner, but Jesus!

You might be right, they might be better off without me,
   but Jesus!

You might be right, I could deserve to die, but Jesus![18]

Feel the Bottom

Charles Spurgeon cherished a particular picture. The engraver portrayed the moment in *Pilgrim's Progress* in which Christian panics as he's being swallowed up by the deeps of a river and going under. The portrait shows Christian's companion, Hopeful, pushing up with his arm around Christian and lifting up his hand, shouting, "Fear not! Brother, I feel the bottom."

With this picture in his mind, the preacher so familiar with sorrows rejoices with those listening to him. "This is just what Jesus does in our trials," Spurgeon proclaims. "He puts his arm around us, points up and says, 'Fear not! The water may be deep, but the bottom is good.'"[19]

It may be that you suffer from a mental sickness in the form of depression of spirit. Things look dark, and your heart is heavy. Life is like a foggy day. Providence is cloudy and stormy, and you are caught in a hurricane. Your soul is exceedingly sorrowful, and you are bruised as a cluster trodden in the winepress. Yet cling close to God, and never let go of your reverent fear of him. However exceptional and unusual may be your trial, with Job whisper these words, "Though he slay me, yet will I trust him."

TEN

J. C. RYLE (1816–1900):
Faithful amid Personal Ruin

BEN ROGERS

When J. C. Ryle turned twenty-five in May 1841, he had all the world before him. He was the heir to an immense fortune, including the elegant Henbury estate, a £15,000-a-year income, and properties valued at more than £500,000. He was an accomplished scholar-athlete. While at Oxford he captained the University XI (cricket) and won a number of academic honors, including a brilliant first-class in *Literae Humaniores*.[1] After a brief stint in London reading the law at Lincoln's Inn, he returned to his hometown of Macclesfield, where he was made a county magistrate and the captain of the Cheshire Yeomanry and began preparing for a career in politics. The young Ryle's star was on the rise in the spring and early summer of 1841.

Then the unthinkable happened.

His father, John Ryle Jr., owned two banks. The Maccles-field branch was founded in 1810, and a second branch was opened in Manchester in 1821. Though the Macclesfield branch prospered, the Manchester branch was poorly su-pervised by the partners and left in the hands of an unwise manager who had a penchant for making bad loans and even worse investments. The news of the bank's bad debts reached London, and Ryle's banking associates stopped payment and refused to accept notes from his banks. When word reached Manchester and Macclesfield, panic ensued, and there was a run on the banks. Both branches fell overnight. J. C. Ryle later poignantly explains the significance of that fateful day: "We got up one summer's morning, with all the world before us as usual, and went to bed that same evening completely and entirely ruined."[2]

Bitterness of Bankruptcy

Limited liability was not applied to the banking industry until 1858, and thus everything had to be sold to pay the creditors. Henbury was sold immediately with everything in it. The household servants and staff were dismissed. The children were sent to live with relatives and left with noth-ing but their personal property and clothes. And the young Ryle was forced to sell his two horses, Yeomanry uniform, sword, saddle, and accoutrements for money to live on. In sum, "Everything was swept clean away."[3] Over the next twenty years, both father and son made payments to settle the debts of the bank. The last payment of nine-thirty-seconds of a penny was made in 1861. Ryle went around in threadbare clothing to save as much money as he could to pay off his father's debt—a debt for which he was not legally or morally responsible.

There were social as well as financial repercussions. Bankruptcy was a criminal offense in Victorian England, and bankrupts were regarded as crooks. It brought shame and disgrace on family and friends as well as the offender himself. For that reason, most of the Ryles' family and friends kept their distance for fear of being tainted by the family's ruin. They stood aloof—silent, shocked, and stunned. The young Ryle, whose future seemed so bright, felt the weight of the fall deeply. He says:

> To be suddenly turned out of a place which on many accounts I liked extremely, and where I had hoped to live and die; to be sent away from a country in which I was born, and had attained some position; to have the whole of my plans and prospects in life in a moment smashed, broken up, and shivered to pieces; to be compelled in a moment to give up all my intentions, and to choose some entirely new life to live; to be reduced from thorough independence in money matters, to such thorough poverty, that I have often hardly known how to get on; to be obliged at the age of 25 to descend from the terms of equity in which I had lived with scores of people, and feel I was no longer able to live on terms of equality with them, and was in fact not much better off than their butlers and footmen; and have the deep and abiding conviction the best thing I could do was to get away from every one I had ever seen, and never see them anymore; to bury myself in some distant part of England, and try to form new acquaintances and new friendships and drop the old ones; all this was a very bitter cup to drink.[4]

Though modern readers may not share Ryle's Victorian assumptions about class and equity, his distress is palpable. He later speculated that if he had not been a Christian he may have committed suicide.

Ryle never explained precisely how his faith saw him through the terrible summer of 1841. He was a notoriously private person and rarely spoke about his inward spiritual conflicts. He would, however, write in his autobiography about the spiritual lessons he learned, and there he points out three of them.

Lesson 1: "It was the right thing."

One of the more surprising features of the account of his father's bankruptcy was Ryle's discussion of its cause. Though he acknowledged that his father made a disastrous loan to his brother-in-law and wasn't well suited to banking, the ultimate cause of his ruin was spiritual. He explains:

> I myself had no part whatever in the matter, and knew nothing whatever of the internal affairs of the bank. I suspected my father was uncomfortable for two or three years before the crash came, but he never told me anything about it. I certainly cannot say I was surprised as much as some, and simply because I was a Christian I had long been vexed with the Sabbath-breaking which took place in connextion with the bank, visits to partners, and consultations about worldly business, and the like, and I had a strong presentiment that such a complete departure from my Grandfather's godly ways, would sooner or later be severely chastised.[5]

By all accounts Ryle's grandfather, John Ryle Sr., was a remarkable man. He became a successful silk manufacturer and prosperous landowner. When he died in 1808, he left his son, John Ryle Jr., somewhere between £250,000 and £500,000.[6] John Sr.'s success also extended to the political sphere. He was elected alderman and then mayor of Macclesfield. John was also a committed evangelical Christian, Methodist, and philanthropist. His mother had been converted after hearing John Wesley preach in 1745, and through her influence he became a Christian. Wesley and Ryle became intimate friends, and Wesley often stayed at his home when he visited Macclesfield, which he did regularly from 1759 until his death in 1791. He even preached from Ryle's front door to large crowds gathered on the front lawn.

J. C. Ryle's father inherited his father's wealth, business acumen, and interest in public service but not his evangelical faith. Their home, though happy and comfortable, was destitute of real spiritual religion. Family prayers were almost never said, and the children's spiritual instruction was nearly nonexistent. Moreover, the young John Charles was brought up to regard evangelicals as "well-meaning, extravagant, fanatical enthusiasts, who carried things a great deal too far in religion."[7] So when J. C. Ryle was converted in 1837, his family was horrified and desperately tried to convince him to abandon his new religious principles. Their efforts, however, had quite the opposite effect. Contending for his newly found evangelical faith only rooted him more deeply in it, attached him more firmly to it, and helped turn him into a formidable evangelical apologist. But this sad episode provides a good illustration of the "departure" Ryle mentioned.

Lesson 2: "It was all for the best."

In addition to seeing God's justice in his father's bankruptcy, he also saw God's providence at work. He writes:

> Taking a moral and spiritual view of it, I have not the least doubt it was all for the best. If my father's affairs had prospered, and I had never been ruined, my life of course would have been a very different one. I should probably have gone into Parliament very soon, and it is impossible to say what the effect of this might have been upon my soul. I should have formed different connexions, and moved in an entirely different circle. I should never have been a clergyman, never have preached a sermon, written a tract, or a book. Perhaps I might not have been as useful and might have made a shipwreck in spiritual things.[8]

Within six months of the bankruptcy, Ryle was ordained a clergyman of the Church of England. It may surprise many readers to know that he never had any particular desire to enter the Christian ministry. But with his inheritance gone and his political ambitions dashed, he needed to support himself immediately. The learned professions—law, medicine, and engineering—offered little immediate income, so he entered the church. He later writes, "I became a clergyman because I felt shut up to it, and saw no other course of life open to me."[9]

Though Ryle's "calling" to ministry is somewhat anomalous by New Testament standards, he quickly gained a reputation for being a powerful preacher, diligent pastor, popular author, and effective polemicist. He rose through the evangelical ranks to become the undisputed leader and party spokesman—the first to hold that distinction since Charles Simeon. He became the first bishop of Liverpool in 1880, at an age when many clergymen contemplate retirement, and served as the chief pastor of the second city (Liverpool) of the British Empire until his death in 1900.

Spiritual usefulness—doing good to souls—and not personal advancement was always Ryle's top pastoral priority. It is the common thread that runs throughout his many and various works. Testimonies to the usefulness of Ryle's ministry abound. Henry Lakin, "a notorious publican" living in Stapenhill, became concerned about his soul after hearing the preaching of a zealous colporteur (a person who distributes Bibles). Even though he never met Ryle, he knew him from his tracts and wrote to him for advice. Ryle penned an encouraging reply and sent him a Bible and a number of tracts, which led to his eventual conversion. Canon W. J. Knox-Little, a ritualist clergyman and opponent of Ryle and his party, tells the Swansea Church Congress in 1879:

> When I was a lad awakening to the deeper thoughts of spiritual things . . . groping about in the dark for something to get hold of, it was one of those beautiful tracts of Canon Ryle's that was my guide, and as long as I live I shall respect and love him for the sake of the tract that did me so much good.[10]

The most memorable of these accounts may be the conversion of a Dominican priest who read one of Ryle's tracts on his way to stamp out a reform movement in the church in Mexico. He was converted after reading the tract and continued on to foster the movement he originally intended to destroy. The Protestant church born as a result grew to more than forty thousand members by the end of the nineteenth century. Even years after Ryle's death, his successor in Liverpool, Bishop F. J. Chavasses, received letters from all over the world thanking Ryle for the spiritual guidance his writings provided. Testimonies such as these could be easily multiplied.

Perhaps the greatest tribute to J. C. Ryle's spiritual usefulness came from Canon Richard Hobson. In his funeral tribute to his late bishop he says:

> A great man has just now fallen in Israel, in the decease of the dear Bishop. Yes, he was great through the abounding grace of God. He was great in stature; great in mental power; great in spirituality; great as a preacher and expositor of God's most holy Word; great in hospitality; great in winning souls to God; great as a writer of Gospel tracts; great as a writer of works which will long live; great as a Bishop of the Reformed Evangelical Protestant Church in England, of which he was a noble defender; great as first Bishop of Liverpool. I am bold to say, that perhaps few men in the nineteenth century did as much for God, for truth, and for righteousness, among the English speaking race, and in the world, as our late Bishop.[11]

And yet none of this great and useful work would have been done if Ryle had never been ruined by his father's bankruptcy. From a moral and spiritual point of view, the bankruptcy really was "all for the best." It propelled him into the Christian ministry and on to great usefulness in Christ's service. The destruction of Ryle's worldly ambition was the salvation of many souls.

Lesson 3: "Troubles in fact not felt are no troubles at all."

A third lesson Ryle learned from the family's ruin was about suffering and submission to the will of God. He explains:

> I believe that God never expects us to feel no suffering or pain when it pleases Him to visit us with affliction. There are great mistakes upon this point. Submission to God's will is perfectly compatible with intense and keen suffering under the chastisements of that will. Troubles in fact not felt are no troubles at all. To feel trouble deeply, and yet submit to it patiently is that which is required of a Christian. A man may submit cheerfully to a severe surgical operation, in the full belief that it is his duty to submit, and that the operation is the likeliest way to secure health. But it does not follow that he does not feel the operation most keenly, even at the moment that he is most submissive. It was a wise saying of holy Baxter when he was dying of a painful disease, "I groan, but I do not grumble." I ask my children and anyone who may read this Autobiography not to forget this. I ask them to remember that I felt most acutely my father's ruin, my exile from Cheshire with the destruction of all my worldly prospects, and I have never ceased to feel them from that day to this; but I would have them know, that I was submissive to God's will, and had a firm and deep conviction that all was right, though I could not see it, and feel it at the time.[12]

The summer of 1841 would not be the last time Ryle experienced "intense and keen" suffering. The transition from riches to rags remained a perpetual trial: "I never felt so utterly what a miserable thing it is, for a man to be first rich, and then poor."[13]

In November 1843 he was forced to resign the curacy of Exbury (his first ministry position) due to illness after ministering there less than two years. He blamed it on the climate of the district, but his symptoms—"constant headache, indigestion, and disturbances of the heart"[14]—are consistent with anxiety or depression, which may have been caused by isolation, overwork, a lack of rest, and grief over his recent personal losses.

Faithfulness Tinged with Tragedy

When he accepted the call to Helmingham in 1844, he finally achieved some degree of financial independence and personal happiness. He was married to Matilda Plumptre in 1845, and their only child, Georgina Matilda Ryle, was born two years later. But shortly thereafter Matilda became ill, and she died in June 1848.

In the following years death continued to make "great gaps" in his circle of friends and family. He lost his mother, sister, brother-in-law, and many of his best friends in the 1850s. His second wife, Jessie Elizabeth Walker, lost her mother, father, sister, and brother during the same time period.

The worst trial of all was Jessie's continued illness. She became ill less than six months after her marriage to Ryle in 1850 and remained infirm for the majority of their ten-year marriage. She gave birth to five children during this time: Isabella (1851), Reginald (1854), Herbert (1856), and Arthur (1857). She also birthed an unnamed daughter who was either stillborn or died shortly after birth in 1853. Jessie died of Bright's disease in 1860, and Ryle was left a widower—for a second time—with five children ranging in age from three to thirteen. These were years of intense, seemingly endless trials. More personal tragedies and disappointments followed. Ryle's eldest child, Georgina, suffered from long-term mental illness and spent most of her life confined to asylums. He was married for a third time in 1861 to Henrietta Clowes, and they had a long and happy marriage. But he outlived her as well, and her death in 1889 was a devastating blow to the then Bishop of Liverpool.

The spiritual lives of his children also proved to be a source of deep disappointment. Only one of his five children (Isabella) embraced his evangelical faith. Arthur and Reginald never made professions of faith. Herbert seemed to follow in his father's footsteps for a season. After university, he entered the ministry and even served as an examining chaplain to his father for a time (1883–87). But he embraced higher-critical views of the Old Testament—views his father utterly abhorred—and had to step down. It was another devastating blow to Bishop Ryle in the latter years of his ministry.

It should also be remembered that Ryle was hounded by critics throughout his long ministry. High churchmen and ritualists criticized his outspoken evangelical Protestantism. Dissenters attacked his attachment to the Church of England. Members of his own party condemned him for his willingness to work with nonevangelical churchmen toward church reform. And this is to say nothing of the near incessant criticism he received for his episcopal leadership.

J. C. Ryle's ministry from beginning to end was marked by suffering, but his ministry was also shaped by it in important ways. Personal losses and crosses, as well as his regular ministry to the sick and dying, served as powerful reminders of the nearness of death, judgment, and eternity. These themes appear repeatedly throughout his works. Moreover, his distinctive simplicity and directness, boldness and urgency, as well as his focus on "things needful for salvation," was informed and to some degree developed in response to his regular and repeated brushes with suffering, sickness, and death. Suffering also helped him develop a tenderness and pastoral sensitivity that often goes unnoticed and unappreciated. He compiled and published a number of small hymnbooks for the encouragement of invalids in his parish, and he wrote a number of tracts for the sick and the dying as well as for those who ministered to them. One of the great themes of these pastoral works is quiet and trusting submission to the will of God—a lesson he first learned through bankruptcy.

Conclusion

When the Ryle family banks crashed in the summer of 1841, the family was ruined, social ties were severed, open doors of opportunity were shut, and the young and accomplished J. C. Ryle's political career was over before it started. But a minister was born. If Bishop Ryle had never been bankrupt, there would be no sermons, no tracts, no biographies, no *Holiness: Its Nature, Hindrances, Difficulties, and Roots*, no *Expository Thoughts on the Gospels*, and none of his other works that remain popular with a wide swath of evangelicals today, and this is to say nothing of the immense good he did for the many souls under his care as a curate, rector, rural dean, canon, and bishop of Liverpool. In short, no bankruptcy, no *bishop*.

Part of what made (and continues to make) Ryle so useful to so many was his own personal acquaintance with suffering and hardship. The many personal trials Ryle faced throughout his ministry—starting with the bankruptcy that propelled him into ministry in the first place—taught him how to persevere amid suffering, helped both to shape his message and to find his voice as a preacher and writer, and gave him new resources to aid in the cure of souls.

ELEVEN

JANANI LUWUM (1922–77): Faithful unto Death

DIEUDONNÉ TAMFU

Death brings life. That is the definition of Christianity. First, the founder of our faith brought us life through his death. Then, the early church delivered the gospel of Christ to the world and to us through the blood of martyrs. The gospel was born in blood, and it survives and spreads through blood until the return of the King, who died to bring life to all who trust in him.

Physical death is not the only means of evangelism. The apostles spread the gospel throughout the world before they became martyrs. But they faced death daily. Paul famously declares, "I die every day!" (1 Cor. 15:31). In 2 Corinthians 4:8–11, he describes the daily death of the apostles:

> We are afflicted in every way, but not crushed; perplexed, but not driven to despair; persecuted, but not forsaken; struck

down, but not destroyed; always carrying in the body the death of Jesus, so that the life of Jesus may also be manifested in our bodies. For we who live are always being given over to death for Jesus' sake, so that the life of Jesus also may be manifested in our mortal flesh.

Those who die daily bring the life of Jesus to others. Death to the comforts of this life, death to physical and financial security—these daily deaths prepare the Christian's heart for martyrdom, the most noble suffering, so that he can face it with joy. Such was the case for Janani Luwum, an Anglican archbishop who faithfully died daily until the day of his death.

Road Prepared with Blood

In 1877 a team of Protestant missionaries arrived in Uganda and were welcomed by the king, Kabaka Mutesa. In 1885, Anglican missionary James Hannington attempted to enter the country but before he could do so King Mwanga II ordered his execution because of a local prophecy that an invader was coming from the east to "devour" Uganda. Hannington's last words were, "I am now going to die at your hands . . . but I want you to tell your king that my blood has bought this way into Uganda." He became the first bishop martyr in Uganda.[1]

Others who embraced faith in Jesus became a stench to King Mwanga II. He accused them of treason because they would not approve his sexually immoral practices. In 1886, he gave orders to kill more than forty Christians. By that time, believers had become known as the *praying ones*. In

May 1886 the praying ones were tied up and executed. The older saints encouraged the younger during the execution, saying, "Do not be afraid. Our Christian friends are with the Lord. We shall join them." These saints walked to their deaths singing hymns and praying for those who persecuted them. Their executioners were amazed that they faced death as though it were a celebration. The courage of these saints inspired many to seek the Christ in whom these praying ones found so much joy and strength. Their blood also proved indelibly that Christianity was African; it was not merely a religion from the West. Thus, the seed of the gospel was sown through blood in Uganda.

Luwum's Life and Ministry

Following in the footsteps of the praying ones, Janani Luwum suffered under an oppressive Ugandan president, Idi Amin, and was killed for calling out the president's atrocities.

Janani Luwum was born in 1922 at Acholi, Uganda. He was born of Christian parents who were converted through a missionary's labors. Though originally from a humble background as a farmer, over time Luwum's father gained prominence as a Christian teacher. As a child Luwum worked on his parents' farm, shepherding cattle, sheep, and goats. Because his parents were poor, he could not attend school until the age of ten, when he attended a school in Gulu. Later, he would become a leader of this institution. After secondary school, Luwum attended a training school and became a teacher.

In 1947, Luwum married his wife, Mary. She was an excellent supporter during his years of ministry. They had several children who with their mother fled Uganda for safety after Luwum was murdered.

In early 1948, Luwum was converted to Christ during the great East African Revival. Immediately, he started preaching. He testifies about these early years:

> When I was converted, after realizing that my sins were forgiven and the implications of Jesus's death and resurrection, I was overwhelmed by a sense of joy and peace. I suddenly found myself climbing a tree to tell those in the school compound to repent and turn to Jesus Christ. From time to time I spoke in tongues. I stayed up that tree for a long time. Later on I discovered that some boys were converted due to a sermon I preached up that tree. The reality of Jesus overwhelmed me— and it still does. But I would be wrong to demand that those who are converted should climb a tree and speak in tongues.[2]

This child of the revival was captivated by the glory of God in the face of Christ.

In December 1948, almost a year after his conversion, Luwum sensed a call to ministry and surrendered his life to serving the church. Although he had early aspired to become a chief among the Acholi tribe, he traded that goal for the great call to serve Christ. However, he never lost interest in the public sphere and political affairs. For him, Christianity did not require renunciation of public or political power but sanctification of them. All his life he advocated for the responsible use of political power. Luwum's passion for justice and equity led to his death.

Luwum became an Anglican deacon in 1954 after studying at St. Augustine's College of Canterbury. In 1956 he was ordained an Anglican priest. In 1969 he was ordained a bishop of northern Uganda. Luwum served in each role faithfully, giving attention to the congregations under his care. Luwum was widely known for his fearless gospel proclamation, and his influence grew immensely, even to an international level. The Anglican churches elected Luwum to be archbishop of the Ugandan church in 1974. He oversaw churches in Uganda, Burundi, and Boga-Zaire. He preached fearlessly, counseled wisely, and boldly addressed political issues. His sermons were filled with everyday stories that illustrated the gospel message.

Luwum's Last Days

From 1894 to 1962 Uganda was a protectorate of Britain. Uganda eventually gained independence from its protectorate on October 9, 1962. Following the declaration of independence, Uganda experienced deadly internal strife.

Uganda's first leader was Bugandan chief Edward Muteesa II. He was succeeded by Milton Obote in 1966. Five years later, Obote was overthrown by Idi Amin in a military coup. Amin wiped out entire tribes, including that of Obote, which he overthrew to gain power over the country. His presidency was characterized by countless deaths and vanishings. Amin never permitted suspected opponents to live. He expelled all Asians from Uganda. He killed many Christians. He was accused of cannibalism and suspected of gross sexual immorality. Amin is considered the African Adolf Hitler.

Luwum confronted this dictator, and his boldness led to his death. He faced Amin with the courage of a lion but died with the meekness of a lamb, bearing the shame and the reproach of his Savior, Jesus Christ.

Facing the Beast

Soon after Luwum was consecrated as archbishop, he faced difficult circumstances in Kampala, Uganda's capital city. While devoting himself to ministry responsibilities, Luwum increasingly attended meetings with Amin's regime. The meetings were so frequent that some accused him of being manipulated by the corrupt leader. But Luwum saw these meetings as opportunities to seek the welfare of Uganda's citizens.

Amin was not always receptive to Luwum's efforts. In August of his first year as archbishop, Luwum began opposing Amin's brutality. When students at Luwum's university protested the murder of one of the university's administrators, Amin's regime responded by beating, raping, and brutalizing students. Luwum chaired a meeting with other religious leaders on August 26, 1976, and they requested a meeting with Amin. The request was rejected. So they wrote a letter to Amin, which reads in part:

> We are deeply disturbed. In the history of our country such an incident in the Church has never before occurred. This is a climax of what has been constantly happening to our Christians. We have buried many who have died as a result of being shot and there are many more whose bodies have not yet been found; yet their disappearance is connected with the activities of some members of the Security Forces. The gun which was meant to protect Uganda as a nation, the Ugandan citizen and his property, is increasingly being used against the Ugandan to take away his life and property.[3]

Even after he helped pen this letter, some continued to accuse Luwum of siding with Amin. In December 1976 he responded with the following message:

I do not know for how long I shall be occupying this chair. I live as though there will be no tomorrow. I face daily being picked up by the soldiers. While the opportunity is there, I preach the gospel with all my might, and my conscience is clear before God that I have not sided with the present government, which is utterly self-seeking. I have been threatened many times. Whenever I have the opportunity I have told the President the things the churches disapprove of. God is my witness.[4]

Luwum condemned Amin and his regime both privately and publicly. In fact, on December 25, 1976, Luwum's radio address was cut off because he was condemning the barbarisms of Amin's regime.

Luwum boldly sought audience with Uganda's most dreaded man. Confronting Amin was playing with death, because corpses fell wherever Amin's shadow was seen. Yet Luwum trusted the gospel that compelled him to protect the lives of innocent citizens and Christians who were being falsely accused and murdered. So he faced the beast.

Sword of the Spirit

Shortly before Luwum's death, Amin sent soldiers to his home. They broke into his home and searched it. They threatened Luwum and commanded him to reveal the weapons he was storing to stage a civil war against Amin. Luwum remained calm. When asked to reveal his weapons, he lifted up his Bible. Luwum told the soldiers it was the only weapon in his home. He explained that he had been praying for President Amin with this weapon that he would rule Uganda in peace and respect for human life. The soldiers didn't touch him that day.

Luwum understood that the battle he was waging was greater than what met the eye. He knew the only effective weapon against the powers of darkness is God's Word, which fueled his prayers. He made the most of this weapon. He did not need guns to oppose the president's outrageous killings. He did not need a machete. He used one weapon, the Word of God, which filled him with the courage to speak and drove him to his knees to pray for Amin and Uganda.

Path of Blood

Festo Kivengere, Anglican bishop of Uganda known as "the Billy Graham of Africa," writes in his book *I Love Idi Amin*:

> Peace is not automatic. It is a gift of the grace of God. It always comes when hearts are exposed to the love of Christ. But this always costs something. For the love of Christ was demonstrated through suffering, and those who experience that love can never put it into practice without some cost.[5]

The peace Luwum longed for would cost him his life.

In 1977 Luwum delivered a final note of protest to Amin against the arbitrary assassinations and mysterious disappearances of many Ugandans. Not long afterward, Amin had him arrested. According to reports, he spent his time in the prison explaining the gospel to prisoners and praying over them. Even though he knew death was looming, Luwum continued to give himself to the work of ministry, faithfully serving his Lord to the point of death.

On February 16, 1977, Luwum was murdered by Amin, whose regime falsely claimed that Luwum died in a car accident.

This was one of Amin's most infamous killings, as Luwum was one of the most influential church leaders in modern Africa and a leading voice of opposition to Amin's tyranny. Author Nancy Mairs reflects on Luwum's execution:

> Having refused to sign a confession, he prayed for his captors as he was undressed and thrown to the floor, whipped, perhaps sodomized, and then at 6:00, shot twice in the chest. Prison vehicles were driven over his body to suggest the automobile accident the government announced the next morning (showing one wrecked car in the newspaper and quite another on television), and then it was sent to the home village for hasty burial.[6]

Apparently Luwum's prayers provoked Amin to charge his men to undress, sodomize, and kill him. It is hard to imagine a more terrible way to die.

We know this is not the end of Luwum's story. Amin thought he was humiliating the archbishop by charging his men to sexually abuse him, but he was actually preparing Luwum for great honor from his God. "Now if we are children, then we are heirs—heirs of God and co-heirs with Christ, if indeed we share in his sufferings in order that we may also share in his glory" (Rom. 8:17 NIV). This child of God surely shared in Christ's suffering. Jesus was also tormented. Jesus's nakedness was exposed on the cross. Because Luwum suffered the same reproach, great glory awaited him.

Grains of Wheat

Hebrews 13:7 gives us this command: "Remember your leaders, those who spoke to you the word of God. Consider the outcome of their way of life, and imitate their faith." I would apply this verse to leaders both living and dead.

We have considered the outcome of Luwum's way of life and his faith—how he taught Christ's people the Word and sought the lost, how he did not shrink from telling Amin what the Bible says about leadership, how he did not hold back from speaking God's Word to his fellow prisoners and captors. Luwum is one to be remembered and imitated.

Jesus says, "Unless a grain of wheat falls into the earth and dies, it remains alone; but it if dies, it bears much fruit" (John 12:24). Luwum's death resulted in a great revival of Christianity in Uganda and around the world. About five thousand people gathered for his burial next to Hannington's grave. In Nairobi, Kenya, about ten thousand people gathered for his funeral. Later that year, thousands gathered in Uganda's capital city to celebrate the advent of the gospel in their country. Among them were many who had walked away from the faith but who were restored when they heard of Archbishop Luwum's courageous death. His death brought life to many.

We are called to follow leaders like Luwum. Following him means we die daily so that our lives have eternal significance. Luwum's life was marked by death and dying. Luwum died to the hope of a better life on earth; he died to the hope of security on earth; he died to worldly comforts such as family and freedom—he surrendered them all. But in his death, he lived, and his life bears much fruit.

Our Lord initiated our faith through agonizing pain. The gospel has advanced through the suffering and death of its ministers. Luwum and others have followed in the path of blood. Would you too willingly, joyfully, and with confidence walk that glorious path?

Faith Holds One Weapon

God has entrusted the church with a weapon in the inspired Word of God. It was the apostles' defense against the enemy of their faith, and it was Luwum's against the devil behind Amin's rule. When confronted by Amin's forces, Luwum perhaps had Paul's words in mind: "Though we walk in the flesh, we are not waging war according to the flesh. For the weapons of our warfare are not of the flesh but have divine power to destroy strongholds" (2 Cor. 10:3–4). Luwum shone light on the darkness of Amin's regime and brought salvation to many by powerfully wielding this sword.

We have learned that when Luwum was arrested he prayed for other prisoners and ultimately for his captors as they were about to kill him. In praying the Word for his captors, Luwum followed his master, Jesus, who appealed to God's mercy at his death, "Father, forgive them, for they know not what they do" (Luke 23:34). Thus, he overcame evil with good.

This is a man of whom the world was not worthy. You may be wondering what you would have done if you were in Luwum's place. Would you have confronted the corrupt president? Would you have given up your life for your fellow citizens? Would you have focused on the salvation of others in your last days and moments? You may be thinking, *How could I ever have his courage?*

The courage to die for Christ begins long before the moment of martyrdom. That courage is born when you embrace Jesus's call to take up your cross and follow him daily. It is a courage that grows as you wield God's Word. It is a courage refreshed by the Holy Spirit, who daily empowers you to die to self, to pray for those who persecute you, and to even die like your Savior. This is the courage that changes the world.

Often, it is difficult to speak out against falsehood or injustice when you know the cost could be steep. But Luwum displayed the courage of saying hard things—he could have abdicated, but he didn't. Like our Lord Jesus Christ at his trial, Luwum spoke the truth and paid the price. For this he serves as a Christ-honoring model of the high price of truth.

In Janani Luwum we have seen a model of faithfulness. Let us consider the outcome of his way of life and imitate his faith. He remained faithful unto death. Let us have the same resolve as Luwum, who said at his conversion, "Today I have become a leader in Christ's army. I am prepared to die in the army of Jesus. As Jesus shed his blood for the people, if it is God's will, I will do the same."[7]

TWELVE

WANG MING-DAO (1900–1991): Faithful amid Political Coercion

JOHN GILL

All people suffer through various hardships, and Christians are by no means exempt. While Christians might wonder why they suffer for no apparent reason, they must continue to "trust in the Lord without the slightest shadow of doubt, uneasiness or fear. What is the basis for this radical trust in God? It's because of God's love shown through Christ's redemptive work. Such a loving God would not hurt his children."[1]

This exhortation for Christians to suffer well in light of their standing before God was written in the mid-1900s by a Chinese pastor named Wang Ming-Dao. He was no stranger to suffering, facing numerous difficulties throughout his life. The most significant hardship he faced was government-led religious persecution. As a pastor who encouraged Christians to suffer well, one might presume that Wang remained faithful in the midst of persecution.

But he did not. At one point, he abdicated, a surprising but encouraging story that will be told later in this chapter. His failure to withstand compromise was public and even noticed by Christians outside of China. Still, by God's grace it proved to be no barrier to later effectiveness in ministry. In the aftermath of his unfaithfulness, Wang found restoration in Christ. The words he had written earlier in life still rang true—he could trust in the Lord who had redeemed him. Therefore, Wang's life is not a simple story of unwavering faithfulness but one characterized by uncompromising faith in both belief and practice, a comparatively uncharacteristic collapse in his faith, and dependence on Christ's forgiveness in restoration.

Wang shows us that even when we cave to pressure and are unfaithful, God can still faithfully use weak men for his glory.

Who Was Wang Ming-Dao, and Why Is He Important?

Biographer Thomas Alan Harvey called Wang "the Dean of the House Churches" in China.

Wang had an itinerant ministry throughout China, visiting twenty-four of the twenty-eight provinces and taking the pulpit in churches of thirty different denominations. Wang was often absent from his own church for six months of the year. The massive spread of house churches in China in the 1940s and 50s owes to Wang's work. But his early years did not foretell such a godly legacy.

Wang was born in the midst of the Boxer Rebellion, a violent uprising against colonialism in China. His family sought refuge in the Legation Quarter, a refuge for foreigners and Chinese Christians. The apparent hopelessness of the situation led Wang's father, Wang Dzu-Hou, to commit suicide not long after being besieged by the Boxers. He left behind his pregnant wife, Li Wun-I, and one daughter. Wang was born approximately one month after his father's death. Wang manifested intellectual gifts from a young age, and he excelled at a primary school established by the London Missionary Society. Though he grew up attending a Christian church with his family, Wang was not converted until 1914, under the discipleship of an older peer. By 1919 Wang was teaching at a Presbyterian primary school in Baoding, approximately one hundred miles from Beijing.

Wang's theological and ministerial development was significant in shaping a ministry that exhibited profound courage. There were seasons in which Wang paid the price for maintaining his convictions. For example, in 1920 Wang came to believe that biblical baptism was by immersion. Though some in his Presbyterian school attempted to convince him otherwise, Wang would not budge from his newfound conviction. Warned that he would not be able to teach at the boarding school if he continued to espouse believer's baptism by immersion, Wang refused to compromise. Wang lost not only his job but also an opportunity to continue his studies abroad. Though he was greatly discouraged by these losses, Wang began preaching at various conventions and evangelistic campaigns in 1923.

Later that year, Wang began a Bible study at his home, a work that was essentially a house church. It would grow to be established as the Beijing Christian Tabernacle in 1937.

Wang's ministry focused on two fundamentals: "On the one hand I emphasize beliefs; on the other hand I emphasize the Christian's manner of life."[2] Wang was admittedly strict when it came to doctrine and practice, which led him to be criticized by other Christian leaders. He writes, "Since I do not tolerate sin, I have acquired many friends. I have also acquired enemies."[3] Wang argued that Christians should not fear criticism or persecution. They should pay no heed to reputation in the eyes of others and even be willing to lay down their lives. Fear of suffering would surely lead to compromise of God's truth. For most of his life, Wang steadfastly practiced what he preached.

Wang understood his pastoral ministry as a type of prophetic ministry, "to be a trumpet call to the world and on the other hand to be a trumpet call to the church," and that this work would "inevitably provoke opposition and bring attacks" upon himself.[4] In light of the suffering and hardships pastors must endure, Wang gave five guidelines to follow. First, a pastor must resolve to know and follow God's will. Second, he must love his congregation as a parent loves her children. The third and fourth points are two sides of the same coin: a pastor must not entertain thoughts of personal gain or glory; rather, he must be humble and teachable. Finally, a pastor should neither think too highly of personal honor nor fear criticism.[5] His developing views and ministry reflected a high view of doctrinal and ecclesiological purity.

Suffering and God's Will

Wang did not convey the Christian life as devoid of suffering, and he connected our circumstances with God's sovereign will. In his sermon "Accepting God's Will," he presented the following progression: (1) the Christian suffers some hardship, (2) God does not reveal a reason for nor remove the suffering, and (3) the Christian is tempted to respond to God with frustration and anger.[6] Such suffering should be doubly expected by those in ministry.

Wang gives a number of examples of how Christians might suffer, such as when people turn against you, the loss of a loved one, an illness without any cure in sight, and the depression and misery that often accompany incurable maladies. Wang recognized how these types of suffering tempt believers, even pastors, to bear a grudge against God.

> You feel downcast and even broken-hearted. . . . You feel that the Lord has deliberately made you to bear the one thing that is most difficult to bear. . . . You ask in your heart, "What is the meaning of this?" . . . Your heart is filled with darkness and affliction.[7]

Amid suffering, the Christian should trust in God's goodness, as most clearly shown through the redemptive work of Christ. While human suffering and the exhortation to look to Christ are shared by all Christians, Wang recognized how pastors in particular are prone to suffering.

Wang was no stranger to affliction. He lived through various hardships, common and uncommon. He also communicated a biblical theology of suffering to his fellow Christians. While this background serves to make his later failure all the more surprising, it should also help us to see that the overall pattern of his life and ministry was one of faithfulness. His failure was a thread in his life, not the whole tapestry.

Persecution under Japanese Occupation

Wang's faithfulness to Christ was challenged in a new way when faced with oppression from the Japanese occupation. His courage and lack of compromise was encouraging, given the numerous Chinese churches who placed themselves under the influence of the Japanese government.

In 1937 Beijing fell to Japanese forces during the Second Sino-Japanese War. Wang's encounters and interactions with Japanese occupiers are a testimony of faithfulness during uncertain times. In 1939 the Japanese Ministry of Information required all publications, including newspapers and magazines, to publish patriotic slogans supporting the Japanese military. The *Spiritual Food Quarterly*, which Wang had written and edited for more than a decade, faced a stark choice: be a political tool or shut down. Refusal to publish patriotic slogans would not only hurt the publication but also present a danger to Wang's personal well-being. After an initial bout of fear, Wang decided to continue publishing without the slogans. To his surprise he was never arrested, and the *Spiritual Food Quarterly* continued without propaganda for eight years.

The Japanese occupation also threatened local churches. The North China Christian Federation Promotion Committee was established by 1942, and Wang was pressured to lead his congregation into the fold or "subsequently encounter difficulties."[8] Wang gave two reasons for rejecting these overtures. First, Wang believed many false Christians had already joined the organization, and he refused to be yoked to it. Second, he refused due to his suspicion that the Japanese government was seeking to influence Chinese churches. Wang's refusal to compromise reflects the difficult burden a faithful pastor must carry:

Our continued existence as a church depended on our joining [the organization]. I had the feeling that I and my col-
leagues were like the captain and first and second officers of
a steamer, that the vessel was whipped by violent gales and
buffeted by heavy seas, and that the safety or otherwise of
the whole ship (the whole church) depended entirely on us
few officers. Our responsibility was heavy in the extreme; we
only needed to make one mistake and the whole ship would
be plunged to the bottom of the sea.[9]

To reject the overtures of the Japanese government could
mean the congregation of hundreds of believers would no
longer be able to worship together, but to accept would be to
ignore conscience. Courage to remain faithful in the face of
government persecution did not mean Wang was fearless; he
feared for his own safety. Amid growing pressure to capitu-
late, and to encourage both himself and his congregation, he
preached on the suffering, faithfulness, and protection that
Daniel and his friends faced in Babylon. Such encouragement
was necessary for Wang to stand against the ongoing pressure from Japanese authorities and other Chinese Christians
throughout the occupation. Thankfully, the Beijing Christian
Tabernacle was never taken over or closed down.

Persecution under Communism

With the establishment of the People's Republic of China
in 1949, the Chinese church faced a new set of challenges.
While the earlier dangers of the Japanese occupation arose
from outside the church, Christians now faced persecution
from within. The rise of Communism in China brought with
it the Three-Self Patriotic Movement, a state-sanctioned,

interdenominational Protestant body that sought to tie Chinese Christians to Chinese nationalism through removal of Western influences. Their mantra was "self-governing, self-supporting, self-proclaiming."[10] Their effort to tie together the political and religious spheres is evident in a seven-point proposal presented at the movement's national conference in 1954:

(1) Urge all believers to support the Constitution of the People's Republic of China and make their contribution to socialist construction.

(2) Urge all believers to resist the invasion of imperialism and work for world peace.

(3) Continue patriotic studies among the clergy to totally eradicate the influence of imperialism.

(4) Consolidate self-governing and improve the unity of the church.

(5) Research the problems associated with being self-supporting and help churches to achieve this.

(6) Research the work of self-propagation governed by the principle of mutual respect in order to eliminate the vestiges of imperialist poison and spread the pure gospel.

(7) Implement the love of China and of Christ, encourage patriotism, obey the law, and purify the church.[11]

The Three-Self Patriotic Movement was not passive. It actively pursued political reform within the religious sphere through publications and *accusation meetings*. These meetings took place at various churches joining the Three-Self Patriotic

Movement, at which people denounced various Christian groups and individuals as proponents of Western imperialism.

One Three-Self publication conveys the main purpose and motivation:

> The central task for all Christian churches and groups is to have accusation meetings. What must we accuse? We must accuse imperialists, their servants and other decadent elements hiding inside the Church. . . . Americans sent missionaries all over China in the name of spreading the gospel but their true aim was to gather information as special agents. American imperialists raised a group of "church leaders" to be their faithful lapdogs.[12]

Unlike numerous other Christian churches and organizations in China, the Beijing Christian Tabernacle had never formally associated with Western Christians. Therefore, while other pastors might have felt compelled to join the Three-Self movement, Wang rejected numerous overtures to membership. He could not be successfully accused of being a tool of Western imperialism.

Yet the primary reason he didn't wish to join the Three-Self movement was doctrinal. Many of the leading figures in the movement were modernists—those with a theologically liberal perspective on central matters such as biblical inspiration, the virgin birth, the atonement, the resurrection of Christ, and his second coming. Wang raised all these as reasons for why the modernists were fundamentally different from true believers:

> These people say they are Christians but they do not believe the truth in the Bible that needs to be accepted with faith.

They do not believe that man was directly created by God, that Jesus was born of the virgin, that Jesus died on the cross for our sin, that the body of Jesus was resurrected, that Jesus is coming again.[13]

Wang was strongly convinced of regenerate church membership, and refused to meet with unbelievers in a gathering he saw as existing for believers.[14] Yet Wang's unyielding rejection of the movement was not just over doctrinal differences. He didn't see it merely as a gathering led by unbelievers. He believed they were insidious:

The Three-Self Church is the most effective method used by those outside the Church to destroy the Church from the inside out. Throughout history no one has ever before thought of such a clever way to destroy the Church, but today it has been discovered.[15]

The movement not only posed an external threat to the church but also might be likened to a virus that threatened to kill it from the inside. Ironically, the Three-Self church and Wang each believed the other to be a poison within the church.

For these reasons, Wang rejected numerous overtures from Three-Self leaders to join their movement. Wang believed that the Communist government desired its people to have freedom of religion. At the same time, strict conformity to the Communist agenda was a priority of the Three-Self movement. Wang did little to ingratiate himself to Three-Self leaders by continuing to criticize their liberal theology, criticism that led many churches and individuals to flee the movement.

Soon, the kind suggestions for Wang to join changed to threats and persecution. First, movement leaders isolated Wang by denouncing friends and associates at accusation meetings. Some were arrested for ties to Western imperialism; others folded under the pressure and joined. One of Wang's church members committed suicide after experiencing pressure to denounce Wang at one meeting. From 1951 to 1955, Wang faced growing pressure to give in to compromise. This, along with a growing fear of imprisonment, took its toll.

At last, Wang broke.

First Arrest and Compromise

On the evening of August 7, 1955, two months after publishing his most scathing critique of the Three-Self movement, "We—For the Sake of Faith," [16] Wang, his wife, and other church associates were arrested for being counterrevolutionary. His arrest and subsequent interrogations were dark both circumstantially and spiritually. While many Christians have stood resolute in their faith before persecution and death, this moment set the stage for Wang's greatest failure.

Though he originally received a lengthy prison sentence, Wang was released after little more than a year on September 29, 1956, after confessing to multiple crimes he did not commit. Out of fear of a long imprisonment or death and concern for his wife's well-being, Wang gave in to state interrogators who wished to use him to help unify Chinese Christians under the state church.

On September 30 Wang read a confession, "My Self-Examination," at a large gathering of the Three-Self movement. An American report gives the details:

In his "self-examination" before a Christian audience he emphasizes his "political mistakes," also his failure to cooperate with the Government and with the patriotic movement in the Church, especially in the war effort and in support of socialist construction. He confesses wrong attitudes to the Communist Party and to the liberal church leaders who sought his support. There is no evidence that he made any retraction of Christian faith or repudiated any of his basic theological beliefs.[17]

Released from prison, Wang was unable to enjoy his freedom. One of the conditions of his release was to join the Three-Self church and preach as a part of the movement. He was torn between his ongoing conviction against joining the movement and the fear of returning to prison.

Imprisoned for Life, Yet Liberated

Wang's wife was a faithful support for him during these seasons of inner turbulence. She even advocated before the director of the Religious Affairs Bureau for his release from the conditions placed on him to preach for the movement. About six months after his release, Wang grew convinced he could not fulfill his promise to wed his church to the movement.

Soon after moving from the Beijing Christian Tabernacle, on April 29, 1957, Wang and his wife were rearrested and placed in a detention center, where they remained for six years. In 1963, the final court decisions and sentences were passed:

The accused Wang Mingdao is found guilty of counter-revolutionary crime and is sentenced to life-long imprisonment with all political rights permanently revoked. The accused Liu Jingwen is found guilty of counter-revolutionary crime and is sentenced to fifteen years' imprisonment (from 29 April 1958 to 28 April 1973), with all her political rights revoked for a further five years after release.[18]

Wang's greatest fears had been realized. But reaching the bottom of despair also convinced him that he had been unfaithful to God by lying to preserve his life. Whereas he was once afraid of being executed, staying in prison, and his wife dying in prison, Wang now accepted his lot and retracted the confession he had made under duress. He was able to find a sense of peace through confessing his true beliefs before God and the state. He now sought to speak and act on the truth, no matter the consequences.

Lengthy Torture, Exemplary Faith

From 1957 to 1979 Wang served his sentence in the detention center in Beijing, a mining camp in Datong, and a labor camp in Yingying. Throughout these years, he suffered from deteriorating health and was tortured by fellow inmates. Despite these hardships, Wang's confidence in the Lord grew to a point of openly singing praises in prison, something he would never have done previously. Wang continued to give an honest account of his personal convictions throughout his imprisonment.

Wang was released from prison in 1979, finally rejoining his wife in Shanghai. She had been released by the government in 1974. Wang entertained many international visitors, including Billy Graham. Though the government was concerned about his ongoing influence, he openly shared his struggles and failures with all visitors.

As he wrote in "Accepting God's Will," Wang sought and received forgiveness for his sins. Not only did he experience God's forgiveness in conversion, but he was also restored by God's forgiveness after he faltered. "God had lifted him up again and enabled him to stand, so he was just as joyful now as when he had first believed."[19]

Wang Ming-Dao experienced suffering throughout his pastoral ministry from both Christians and the government. As one who shepherded fellow believers to withstand any temptation to compromise in the face of hardship, he was expected to practice what he taught, and faithfulness to Christ was the pattern of his life. The faithfulness he portrayed throughout his life and ministry stood in stark contrast to his failure under Communist oppression.

Temptation to compromise is not uncommon for those in pastoral ministry. Leaders in the church must always be vigilant to cling to the good news of Jesus Christ, not only as a preventive against sin but also when repentance and restoration are needed when we do fall short. Leaders must be willing to speak the truth, even if it may cost them everything.

Wang's story clearly shows that, even if leaders in the church betray their callings, God is able to write a different ending to their stories.

NOTES

Chapter 1 Paul: Apostle of Pastoral Affliction

1. Quoted in Nancy Guthrie, ed., *Be Still, My Soul: Embracing God's Purpose and Provision in Suffering* (Wheaton: Crossway, 2010), 89. The quote has often been expressed as "It is doubtful whether God can *use* a man greatly until he has hurt him deeply" because the context shows that to be close to Tozer's meaning. The quote comes from Tozer's work *The Root of the Righteous: Tapping the Bedrock of True Spirituality* (1955).

2. Thomas R. Schreiner, *Paul, Apostle of God's Glory in Christ: A Pauline Theology* (Downers Grove, IL: InterVarsity, 2001), 87.

3. John Calvin, *Commentary on 1 and 2 Corinthians*, vol. 20 of *Calvin's Commentaries*, trans. John Pringle (Grand Rapids: Baker, 1999), 110.

4. D. A. Carson, *How Long O Lord? Reflections on Evil and Suffering* (Grand Rapids: Baker Academic, 2006), 81.

5. Schreiner, *Paul*, 96.

6. John Bunyan, "Relation of Bunyan's Imprisonment," in *The Works of John Bunyan*, ed. George Offor, vol. 1 (Carlisle, PA: Banner of Truth, 1991), 53.

7. Schreiner, *Paul*, 96.

8. Paul David Tripp, *New Morning Mercies: A Daily Gospel Devotional* (Wheaton: Crossway, 2014), xx.

9. Schreiner, *Paul*, 96.

10. Ajith Fernando, *The Call to Joy and Pain: Embracing Suffering in Your Ministry* (Wheaton: Crossway, 2007), 105.

11. For a longer exposition of the minister's war with self-glory, see Paul David Tripp, *Dangerous Calling: Confronting the Unique Challenges of Pastoral Ministry* (Wheaton: Crossway, 2012), 167–81.

12. Sarah Eekhoff Zylstra, "Why Pastors Are Committing Suicide," The Gospel Coalition, November 23, 2016, https://www.thegospelcoalition .org/article/why-pastors-are-committing-suicide.

Chapter 2 John Calvin (1509–64): Faithful in Exile

1. Theodore Beza, *The Life of John Calvin* (Darlington, UK: Evangelical Press, 1997), 6–7.

2. John Dillenberger, ed., *John Calvin: Selections from His Writings* (Oxford: Oxford University Press, 1975), 71.

3. Dillenberger, *John Calvin*, 71.

4. John Calvin, *John Calvin: Tracts and Letters*, ed. Jules Bonnet (Carlisle, PA: Banner of Truth, 2009), 4:216.

5. Calvin, *John Calvin: Tracts and Letters*, 4:351.

6. Theodore Beza, *The Life of John Calvin*, trans. Henry Beveridge (Lindenhurst, NY: Great Christian Books, 2012), 73.

7. Calvin, *John Calvin: Tracts and Letters*, 2:77

8. Calvin, *John Calvin: Tracts and Letters*, 2:216.

9. John Calvin, *Commentary on the Psalms*, vol. 4 of *Calvin's Commentaries*, trans. John Pringle (Grand Rapids: Baker, 1999), xxxix.

10. Calvin, *John Calvin: Tracts and Letters*, 4:280–81.

11. Calvin, *John Calvin: Tracts and Letters*, 5:313.

12. For a fuller discussion of Calvin's mission to France and Geneva as a missionary center, see Michael A. G. Haykin and C. Jeffrey Robinson Sr., *To the Ends of the Earth: Calvin's Missional Vision and Legacy* (Wheaton: Crossway, 2014).

13. John Calvin, *Commentary on the Epistles of Paul the Apostle to the Corinthians*, vol. 20 of *Calvin's Commentaries*, trans. John Pringle (Grand Rapids: Baker, 1997), 111.

14. Calvin, *John Calvin: Tracts and Letters*, 4:175.

15. Richard Stauffer, *The Humanness of John Calvin: The Reformer as a Husband, Father, Pastor and Friend*, trans. George Shriver (Vestavia Hills, AL: Solid Ground Books, 2008), 78.

16. For a fuller account of Calvin's mentoring of other pastors in Geneva, see Scott M. Manetsch, *Calvin's Company of Pastors: Pastoral Care and the Emerging Reformed Church, 1536–1609* (New York: Oxford University Press, 2013).

17. Manetsch, *Calvin's Company of Pastors*, 84.

18. John Calvin, *Institutes of the Christian Religion*, ed. John T. McNeill, trans. Ford Lewis Battles, vol. 1 (Louisville: Westminster John Knox, 1960), 220–21.

Chapter 3 John Bunyan (1628–88): Faithful in Prison

1. John Bunyan, *Grace Abounding to the Chief of Sinners*, in *The Works of John Bunyan*, ed. George Offor, vol. 1 (Carlisle, PA: Banner of Truth, 1991), 6.
2. Bunyan, *Grace Abounding*, 42.
3. John Bunyan, "Relation of Bunyan's Imprisonment," in *Works of John Bunyan*, 53.
4. Bunyan, "Relation of Bunyan's Imprisonment," 48.
5. Bunyan, *Grace Abounding*, 18.
6. Bunyan, *Grace Abounding*, 47.
7. Bunyan, *Grace Abounding*, 17.
8. Bunyan, *Grace Abounding*, 17.
9. John Bunyan, *Come and Welcome to Jesus Christ*, in *Works of John Bunyan*, 240–41.

Chapter 4 Jonathan Edwards (1703–58): Faithful to the End

1. Jonathan Edwards, *The End for Which God Created the World*, in *Ethical Writings*, ed. Paul Ramsey, vol. 8 of *Works of Jonathan Edwards* (New Haven: Yale University Press, 1989), 526.
2. Jonathan Edwards, "God Glorified in Man's Dependence," in *Sermons and Discourses 1730–1733*, ed. Mark Valeri, vol. 17 of *Works of Jonathan Edwards* (New Haven: Yale University Press, 1999), 202.
3. Jonathan Edwards, "To the Reverend Thomas Gillespie," in *Letters and Personal Writings*, ed. George S. Claghorn, vol. 16 of *Works of Jonathan Edwards* (New Haven: Yale University Press, 1998), 350.
4. Jonathan Edwards, "To the Reverend Thomas Prince," in *Letters and Personal Writings*, 121.
5. Jonathan Edwards, "To the Reverend Thomas Foxcroft," in *Letters and Personal Writings*, 284.
6. David Hall, *The Diary of David Hall* (Boston: MS in Massachusetts Historical Society), quoted in George M. Marsden, *Jonathan Edwards* (New Haven: Yale University Press, 2003), 353.
7. John Piper and Justin Taylor, *A God Entranced Vision of All Things: The Legacy of Jonathan Edwards* (Wheaton: Crossway, 2004), 135.
8. Jonathan Edwards, "A Farewell Sermon," in *Sermons and Discourses 1743–1758*, ed. Wilson Kimnach. vol. 25 of *Works of Jonathan Edwards* (New Haven: Yale University Press, 2006), 483.
9. Jonathan Edwards, "To the Reverend William McCulloch," in *Letters and Personal Writings*, 358.

Chapter 5 John Newton (1725–1807): Faithful amid Disappointment

1. D. Bruce Hindmarsh, *John Newton and the English Evangelical Tradition: Between the Conversions of Wesley and Wilberforce* (Grand Rapids: Eerdmans, 2001), 112.

2. Hindmarsh, *John Newton*, 98.

3. *Hymns of Grace* (Los Angeles: The Master's Seminary, 2015), 63.

4. Tony Reinke, *Newton on the Christian Life: To Live Is Christ* (Wheaton: Crossway, 2015), 195, emphasis added.

5. *Hymns of Grace*, 89.

Chapter 6 Andrew Fuller (1754–1815): Faithful amid Heartbreak

1. A number of recent monographs have focused on the Baptist preacher, including Paul Brewster, *Andrew Fuller: Model Pastor-Theologian*, Studies in Baptist Life and Thought (Nashville: B&H Academic, 2010), and Peter J. Modern, *The Life and Thought of Andrew Fuller (1754–1815)*, Studies in Evangelical History and Thought (Milton Keynes, UK: Paternoster, 2015). In addition, a critical edition of the works of Andrew Fuller has begun under the leadership of series editor Michael A. G. Haykin. The series, *The Complete Works of Andrew Fuller*, is under way from the German academic publisher Walter de Gruyter.

2. Cited in Gilbert Laws, *Andrew Fuller: Pastor, Theologian, Ropeholder* (London: The Carey Press, 1942), 127. The quote comes from a "Thank You" letter from Spurgeon to Andrew Gunton Fuller for a copy of his biography on his father in Andrew Gunton Fuller, *Andrew Fuller: Men Worth Remembering* (London: Hodder and Stoughton, 1882). The letter was used in advertisements for the Fuller volume in subsequent publications by Hodder and Stoughton. See William Mackergo Taylor, *John Knox* (London: Hodder and Stoughton, 1884), 215.

3. Jonathan Edwards, *A Careful and Strict Enquiry into the Modern Prevailing Notions of That Freedom of Will, Which is Supposed to be Essential to Moral Agency, Virtue and Vice, Reward and Punishment, Praise and Blame* (Boston: S. Kneeland, 1754).

4. Andrew Fuller, *The Gospel of Christ Worthy of All Acceptation: or The Obligations of Men Fully to Credit, and Cordially to Approve, Whatever God Makes Known. Wherein is Considered the Nature of Faith in Christ, and the Duty of Those Where the Gospel Comes in That Matter* (Northampton: T. Dicey & Co., n.d.).

5. Andrew Fuller, *The Diary of Andrew Fuller, 1780–1801*, ed. Michael D. McMullen and Timothy D. Whelan, vol. 1 of *The Complete Works of Andrew Fuller* (Berlin: Walter de Gruyter, 2016), 162.

6. Quotes in remainder of paragraph and extract that follows are from John Ryland, *The Work of Faith, the Labour of Love, and the Patience of Hope, Illustrated; in the Life and Death of the Rev. Andrew Fuller* (London: Button & Son, 1816), 455–58.

7. Quotes in remainder of paragraph and extract that follows are from Ryland, *The Work of Faith*, 458–59.

8. Ryland, *The Work of Faith*, 185.

9. Andrew Gunton Fuller, *The Complete Works of Andrew Fuller: Memoirs, Sermons, Etc.*, ed. Joseph Belcher, vol. 1 (Harrisonburg, VA: Sprinkle Publications, 1988), 621.

10. Ryland, *The Work of Faith*, 460.

11. A. G. Fuller, *Complete Works of Andrew Fuller*, 334.

12. Fuller, *Diary of Andrew Fuller*, 184.

13. Ryland, *The Work of Faith*, 462.

14. Fuller, *Diary of Andrew Fuller*, 184.

15. A. G. Fuller, *Complete Works of Andrew Fuller*, 66.

16. A. G. Fuller, *Complete Works of Andrew Fuller*, 66–67.

17. Ryland, *The Work of Faith*, 468.

18. A. G. Fuller, *Complete Works of Andrew Fuller*, 68.

19. A.G. Fuller, *Complete Works of Andrew Fuller*, 71.

20. A. G. Fuller, *Complete Works of Andrew Fuller*, 69–70.

21. A. G. Fuller, *Complete Works of Andrew Fuller*, 71–72.

22. A. G. Fuller, *Complete Works of Andrew Fuller*, 73, emphasis original.

23. A. G. Fuller, *Complete Works of Andrew Fuller*, 73.

24. Ryland, *The Work of Faith*, 470.

25. A. G. Fuller, *Complete Works of Andrew Fuller*, 390–91.

Chapter 7 Charles Simeon (1759–1836): Faithful Shepherd to Hostile Sheep

1. Charles Simeon, *Memoirs of the Life of the Rev. Charles Simeon: With a Selection from His Writings and Correspondence*, ed. William Carus (London: Hatchard and Son, 1847), 6.

2. Quotes in remainder of paragraph are from Simeon, *Memoirs*, 9.

3. John Berridge, *The Works of the Rev. John Berridge with an Enlarged Memoir of His Life*, ed. Richard Whittingham (London: Simpkin, Marshall and Company, 1838), 418.

4. Simeon, *Memoirs*, 47.

5. Matthew Morrris Preston, *Memoranda of the Rev. Charles Simeon* (London: Richard Watts, 1840), 22.

6. Preston, *Memoranda of the Rev. Charles Simeon*, 40.

7. Simeon, *Memoirs*, 44.

8. Handley Carr Glyn Moule, *Charles Simeon* (London: Methuen & Co., 1892), 41.

9. Simeon, *Memoirs*, 86.

10. Simeon, *Memoirs*, 55.

11. Simeon, *Memoirs*, 73.

12. Simeon, *Memoirs*, 74.

13. John Henry Overton and Frederic Relton, *The English Church from the Ascension of George I to the End of the Eighteenth Century (1714–1800)* (New York: Macmillan Company, 1906), 242.

14. Ian Chapman, "Charles Simeon of Cambridge: A man who faced and overcame rejection in his parish and maintained and acted on a lifelong vision for the Church both in England and Worldwide," *Churchman* 110, no. 2 (1996).

Chapter 8 John Chavis (1763–1838): Faithful in the Face of Racism

1. "A quality, trait, word, phrase, or manner distinctive or taken to be distinctive of black people," *Merriam-Webster's Dictionary*, 11th ed., s.v. "Negroism."

2. Peter P. Hinks, *To Awaken My Afflicted Brethren: David Walker and the Problem of Antebellum Slave Resistance* (University Park, PA: Penn State University Press, 2006), 85; Henry Highland Garnet, *Walker's Appeal: With a Brief Sketch of His Life* (New York: J. H. Tobitt, 1848).

3. "John Chavis to Willie Person Mangum, September 3, 1831," in *The Papers of Willie Person Mangum*, ed. Henry Thomas Shanks, vol. 1 of Publications of the State Department of Archives and History (Winston-Salem, NC: Winston Printing Company, 1950), 412.

4. Edgar W. Knight, "Notes on John Chavis," *The North Carolina Historical Review* 7, no. 3 (July 1930): 336.

5. F. H. Johnston, "Excerpts from the Orange Presbytery," *North Carolina Presbyterian* (1883).

6. "John Chavis to Willie Person Mangum, September 3, 1831," 412.

7. "John Chavis to Willie Person Mangum, September 3, 1831," 413.

8. "John Chavis to Willie Person Mangum, March 10, 1832," in *Papers of Willie Person Mangum*, 507.

9. Mark Noll, "The Negro Question Lies Far Deeper Than the Slavery Question," in *The Civil War as a Theological Crisis* (Chapel Hill: University of North Carolina Press, 2006).

Chapter 9 C. H. Spurgeon (1834–92): Faithful in Sorrow

1. Charles Spurgeon, *The Early Years: 1834–1859*, vol. 1 of *C. H. Spurgeon's Autobiography* (repr.; Edinburgh: Banner of Truth, 1994), 416–17.

2. Quotes in remainder of paragraph are from Spurgeon, *The Early Years*, 416–17.

3. Spurgeon uses this phrase to describe the multiple bouts with depression that leaders in ministry can experience. See *Lectures to My Students*, vol. 1, lecture 11, AGES Digital Library, CD-ROM, http://www.mat.univie.ac.at/~neum/sciandf/spurgeon/spurgeon1.pdf.

4. William Cowper, "God Moves in a Mysterious Way," 1773, public domain.

5. William Cowper, "The Castaway," 1799, public domain.

6. Charles Spurgeon, "Lama Sabachthani?," *Metropolitan Tabernacle Pulpit*, sermon no. 2133, The Spurgeon Arhive, http://archive.spurgeon .org/sermons/2133.php.

7. Charles Spurgeon, "Healing for the Wounded," *New Park Street Pulpit*, vol. 1, sermon no. 53, The Spurgeon Archive, https://archive.spurgeon .org/sermons/0053.php.

8. Spurgeon said, "Some saints are constitutionally depressed and sad." *Sermons of Rev. C. H. Spurgeon*, ed. Godfrey Holden Pike (London: Funk and Wagnalls, 1892), 390, https://books.google.com/books ?id=9NsTAAAAYAAJ.

9. For example, Spurgeon said, "Bodily pain should help us to understand the cross but mental depression should make us apt scholars of Gethsemane." "Gethsemane," *Metropolitan Tabernacle Pulpit*, sermon no. 493, The Spurgeon Archive, http://archive.spurgeon.org/sermons/0493.php.

10. Charles Spurgeon, *Diary, Letters, and Records*, vol. 2 of Spurgeon, *Autobiography*, chap. 50, 234, Charles H. Spurgeon – "Prince of Preachers," http://www.princeofpreachers.org/uploads/4/8/6/5/48652749/chs _autobiography_vol_2.pdf.

11. Charles Spurgeon, "The Exaltation of Christ," *New Park Street Pulpit*, vol. 2, sermon no. 101, The Spurgeon Center, http://www.spur geon.org/resource-library/sermons/the-exaltation-of-christ#flipbook/.

12. Spurgeon, "Healing for the Wounded."

13. Charles Spurgeon, "Joy, Joy, Forever!," *Metropolitan Tabernacle Pulpit*, sermon no. 2146, Spurgeon Gems, http://www.spurgeongems.org /vols34-36/chs2146.pdf; see also, Charles Spurgeon, "Joyful Transformations," *Metropolitan Tabernacle Pulpit*, Internet Christian Library, https ://www.iclnet.org/pub/resources/text/history/spurgeon/web/ss-0025.html.

14. For a thorough discussion of Spurgeon's approach to medicines see Zack Eswine, *Spurgeon's Sorrows: Realistic Hope for those who Suffer from Depression* (Scotland: Christian Focus, 2014), 105–18.

15. Spurgeon, "The Exaltation of Christ."

16. Charles Spurgeon, "A Troubled Prayer," *Metropolitan Tabernacle Pulpit*, sermon no. 741, Spurgeon Gems, http://www.spurgeongems.org /vols13-15/chs741.pdf.

17. Charles Spurgeon, "Fear Not," *New Park Street Pulpit*, sermon no. 156, The Spurgeon Archive, https://archive.spurgeon.org/sermons/0156.php.

18. Eswine, *Spurgeon's Sorrows*, 50.

19. Eric W. Hayden, *Searchlight on Spurgeon: Spurgeon Speaks for Himself* (Pasadena, TX: Pilgrim Publications, 1973), 185.

Chapter 10 J. C. Ryle (1816–1900): Faithful amid Personal Ruin

1. The *Literae Humaniores* was the archetypal humanities course of study, which focused exclusively on the language and literature of the Greeks and Romans—that is, the Classics. The introduction of the examination system in 1800 allowed students to compete for first-, second-, and third-class honors. Eleven first-class honors were awarded in 1837, but the examinations of J. C. Ryle, Arthur Stanley, and Henry Heighton so far exceeded the rest that making a small class of these men was discussed. This achievement remained a source of pride for the rest of Ryle's life.

2. J. C. Ryle, *Bishop J. C. Ryle's Autobiography: The Early Years*, ed. Andrew Atherstone (Carlisle, PA: Banner of Truth Trust, 2016), 88.

3. Ryle, *Bishop J. C. Ryle's Autobiography*, 87.

4. Ryle, *Bishop J. C. Ryle's Autobiography*, 91.

5. Ryle, *Bishop J. C. Ryle's Autobiography*, 88.

6. Today, this inheritance would be worth somewhere between $22,000,000 and $42,000,000 in US dollars.

7. Ryle, *Bishop J. C. Ryle's Autobiography*, 64.

8. Ryle, *Bishop J. C. Ryle's Autobiography*, 92.

9. Ryle, *Bishop J. C. Ryle's Autobiography*, 98.

10. *Report of the Nineteenth Annual Church Congress Held at Swansea* (London: John Hodges, 1879), 397.

11. Richard Hobson, *What Hath God Wrought: An Autobiography* (London: Charles J. Thynne, 1909), 345–46.

12. Ryle, *Bishop J. C. Ryle's Autobiography*, 94–95.

13. Ryle, *Bishop J. C. Ryle's Autobiography*, 105.

14. Ryle, *Bishop J. C. Ryle's Autobiography*, 104.

Chapter 11 Janani Luwum (1922–77): Faithful unto Death

1. Festo Kivengere, *I Love Idi Amin: The Story of Triumph under Fire in the Midst of Suffering and Persecution in Uganda* (London: Marshall, Morgan and Scott, 1977), 10.

2. Mark A. Noll and Carolyn Nystrom, *Clouds of Witnesses: Christian Voices from Africa and Asia* (Downers Grove, IL: InterVarsity, 2011), 114.

3. Mark Water, ed., *The New Encyclopedia of Christian Martyrs* (Alresford, Hampshire: John Hunt, 2001), 911.

4. Noll and Nystrom, *Clouds of Witnesses*, 120.

5. Kivengere, *I Love Idi Amin*, 62.

6. Nancy Mais, "Janani Leads Me to the Cross," in *Martyrs: Contemporary Writers on Modern Lives of Faith*, ed. Susan Bergman (Maryknoll, NY: Orbis Books, 1998), 84.

7. Margaret Ford, *Even Unto Death: The Story of Uganda Martyr Janani Luwum* (Colorado Springs: David C. Cook, 1978), 21.

Chapter 12 Wang Ming-Dao (1900–1991): Faithful amid Political Coercion

1. Wong Ming-Dao, *Spiritual Food: 20 Messages* (Southampton: Mayflower Christian Books, 2000), 59.

2. Wong Ming-Dao, *A Stone Made Smooth* (Southampton: Mayflower Christian Books, 1981), 130.

3. Wong Ming-Dao, *A Stone Made Smooth*, 132.

4. Wong Ming-Dao, *A Stone Made Smooth*, 87.

5. Wong Ming-Dao, *A Stone Made Smooth*, 139.

6. Wong, *Spiritual Food*, 59.

7. Wong, *Spiritual Food*, 59–60.

8. Wong, *Spiritual Food*, 215.

9. Wong, *Spiritual Food*, 217.

10. Wong, *Spiritual Food*, preface.

11. Excerpt of the official report from the Chinese Christian National Conference found in Stephen Wang, *The Long Road to Freedom: The Story of Wang Mingdao* (Kent, England: Sovereign World Ltd., 2002), 49.

12. Wang, *Long Road to Freedom*, 30–31.

13. Wang, *Long Road to Freedom*, 75.

14. "He did not want any division between those who truly believed but he wholeheartedly urged those with real faith to separate themselves from unbelievers." Wang, *Long Road to Freedom*, 73.

15. Wang, *Long Road to Freedom*, 41.

16. Wang Mingdao, "We—For the Sake of Faith," *Occasional Bulletin* 7, no. 3 (March 15, 1956): 1–21.

17. Wang Mingdao, "My Self-Examination," trans. Frank W. Price, *Occasional Bulletin* 8, no. 3 (March 3, 1957): 1–5.

18. Wang, *Long Road to Freedom*, 162.

19. Wang, *Long Road to Freedom*, 220.

Collin Hansen (MDiv, Trinity Evangelical Divinity School) serves as editorial director for The Gospel Coalition. He is the author of *Blind Spots* and *Young, Restless, Reformed*; the co-author of *A God-Sized Vision*; and coeditor with Tim Keller of the CULTURAL RENEWAL series. He previously worked as an associate editor for *Christianity Today* magazine and serves on the advisory board of Beeson Divinity School. He lives in Alabama with his wife, Lauren, and their two children.

Jeff Robinson (PhD, Southern Baptist Theological Seminary) is a senior editor for The Gospel Coalition. He pastors Christ Fellowship Church of Louisville, Kentucky, serves as senior research and teaching associate for the Andrew Fuller Center for Baptist Studies, and is an adjunct professor of church history at Southern Seminary. He is coauthor with Michael Haykin of *To the Ends of the Earth* and coeditor with D. A. Carson of *Coming Home* and with Collin Hansen of *15 Things Seminary Couldn't Teach Me*. He lives in Kentucky with his wife, Lisa, and their four children.

THE GOSPEL **COALITION**

*Advocate for Gospel-Centered
Principles and Practices*

To learn more, visit:
www.TheGospelCoalition.org

LIKE THIS
BOOK?
Consider sharing it with others!

- Share or mention the book on your social media platforms. Use the hashtag **#12FaithfulMen**.

- Write a book review on your blog or on a retailer site.

- Pick up a copy for friends, family, or anyone who you think would enjoy and be challenged by its message.

- Share this message on Twitter or Facebook: **"I loved #12FaithfulMen by @Collin Hansen @ReadBakerBooks"**

- Recommend this book for your church, workplace, book club, or class.

- Follow Baker Books on social media and tell us what you like.

 Facebook.com/ReadBakerBooks

 @ReadBakerBooks